Emile Joseph Dillon

The sceptics of the Old Testament, Job, Koheleth, Agur

Emile Joseph Dillon

The sceptics of the Old Testament, Job, Koheleth, Agur

ISBN/EAN: 9783337736255

Printed in Europe, USA, Canada, Australia, Japan

Cover: Foto ©ninafisch / pixelio.de

More available books at **www.hansebooks.com**

THE SCEPTICS OF THE OLD TESTAMENT

JOB · KOHELETH · AGUR

WITH ENGLISH TEXT TRANSLATED FOR THE FIRST
TIME FROM THE PRIMITIVE HEBREW AS RESTORED ON THE BASIS
OF RECENT PHILOLOGICAL DISCOVERIES

BY

E. J. DILLON

*Late Professor of Comparative Philology and Ancient Armenian at the Imperial
University of Kharkoff; Doctor of Oriental Languages of the University of
Louvain; Magistrand of the Oriental Faculty of the Imperial University
of St. Petersburg; Member of the Armenian Academy of Venice;
Membre de la Société Asiatique de Paris," &c. &c.*

LONDON
ISBISTER AND COMPANY Limited
15 & 16 TAVISTOCK STREET COVENT GARDEN
1895

To

ALEXANDER VASSILYEVITCH PASCHKOFF, M.A.

THE FOLLOWING PAGES

ARE

AFFECTIONATELY DEDICATED

DEDICATORY NOTE

My dear Paschkoff,

In the philosophical problems dealt with by the Sceptics of the Old Testament, you will recognise the theme of our numerous and pleasant discussions during the past sixteen years. Three of these are indelibly engraven in my memory, and, if I mistake not, in yours.

The first took place in St. Petersburg one soft Indian-summer's evening, in a cosy room on the Gagarine Quay, from the windows of which we looked out with admiration upon the blue expanse of the Neva, as it reflected the burnished gold of the spire of the Fortress church. At that time we gazed upon the wavelets of the river and the wonders of the world from exactly the same angle of vision.

The second of these memorable conversations occurred after the lapse of nine years. We had met together in the old place, and sauntering out one bitterly cold December evening resumed the discussion, walking to and fro on the moonlit bank of the ice-bound river, until evening merged into night and the moon sank beneath the horizon, leaving us in total darkness, vainly desirous, like Goethe, of "light, more light."

Our last exchange of views took place after six further years had sped away, and we stood last August on the summit of the historic

DEDICATORY NOTE

Mönchsberg, overlooking the final resting-place of the great Paracelsus. The long and interesting discussions which we had on that occasion, just before setting out in opposite directions, you to the East and I to the West, neither of us is likely ever to forget.

It is in commemoration of these pleasant conversations, and more especially of the good old times, now past for ever, when we looked out upon the wavelets of the Neva and the wonders of the world from the same angle of vision, that I ask you to allow me to associate your name with this translation of the primitive texts of the Sceptics of the Old Testament.

         Yours affectionately,
            E. J. DILLON.

TREBIZOND,
 January 3, 1895.

PREFACE

A CAREFUL perusal of this first English translation of the primitive text of "Job," "Koheleth," and the "Sayings of Agur" will, I doubt not, satisfy the most orthodox reader that I am fully warranted in characterising their authors as Sceptics. The epithet, I confess, may prove distasteful to many, but the truth, I trust, will be welcome to all. It is not easy to understand why any one who firmly believes that Providence is continually educing good from evil should hesitate to admit that it may in like manner allow sound moral principles to be enshrined in doubtful or even erroneous philosophical theories. Or, is trust in God to be made dependent upon the confirmation or rejection by physical science of, say, the Old Testament account of the origin of the rainbow? Agur, "Job" and "Koheleth" had outgrown the intellectual husks which a narrow, inadequate and erroneous account of God's dealings with man had caused to form around the minds of their countrymen, and they had the moral courage to put their words into harmony with their thoughts. Clearly perceiving that, whatever the sacerdotal class might say to the contrary, the political strength of the Hebrew people was spent and its religious ideals exploded, they sought to shift the centre of gravity from speculative theology to practical morality.

The manner in which they adjusted their hopes, fears, and aspirations to the new conditions, strikes the keynote of their respective characters. "Job," looking down upon the world from the tranquil heights of genius, is manful, calm, resigned. "Koheleth," shuddering at the gloom that envelops and the pain that convulses all living beings, prefers death to life, and freedom from suffering to "positive" pleasure; while Agur, revealing the bitterness bred by dispelled illusions and blasted hopes, administers a severe chastisement to those who first called them into being. All three[*] reject the dogma of retribution, the doctrine of eternal life and belief in the coming of a Messiah, over and above which they at times strip the notion of God of its most essential attributes, reducing it to the shadow

---

[*] In Agur's case, this is but an inference from his first saying, but an inference which few would think of calling in question.

of a mere metaphysical abstraction. This is why I call them Sceptics.

"Job" and "Koheleth" emphatically deny that there is any proof to be found of the so-called moral order in the universe, and they unhesitatingly declare that existence is an evil. They would have us therefore exchange our hopes for insight, and warn us that even this is very circumscribed at best. For not only is happiness a mockery, but knowledge is a will-o'-the-wisp. Mankind resembles the bricklayer and the hodman who help to raise an imposing edifice without any knowledge of the general plan. And yet the structure is the outcome of their labour. In like manner this mysterious world is the work of man—the mirror of his will. As his will is, so are his acts, and as his acts are, so is his world. Or as the ancient Hindoos put it:

> "Before the gods we bend our necks, and yet within the toils of Fate
> Entangled are the gods themselves. To Fate, then, be all honour given.
> Yet Fate itself can compass nought, 'tis but the bringer of the meed
> For every deed that we perform.
> As then our acts shape our rewards, of what avail are gods or Fate?
> Let honour therefore be decerned to deeds alone."

But what, I have been frequently asked, will be the effect of all this upon theology? Are we to suppose that the writings of these three Sceptics were admitted into the Canon by mistake, and if not, shall we not have to widen our definition of inspiration until it can be made to include contributions which every Christian must regard as heterodox? An exhaustive reply to this question would need a theological dissertation, for which I have neither desire nor leisure. I may say, however, that eminent theologians representing various Christian denominations — Roman Catholic, Greek Orthodox, Anglican and Lutheran — have assured me that they could readily reconcile the dogmas of their respective Churches with doctrines educible from the primitive text of "Job," "Koheleth," and Agur, whose ethics they are disposed to identify, in essentials, with the teachings of the Sermon on the Mount. With the ways and means by which they effect this reconciliation I am not now concerned.

My object was neither to attack a religious dogma, nor to provoke a theological controversy, but merely to put the latest results of philological science within the reach of him who reads as he runs. And I feel confident that the reader who can appreciate the highest forms of poetry, or who has anxiously pondered over the problems of God, immortality, the origin of evil, &c., will peruse the writings of " Job," " Koheleth " and Agur with a lively interest, awakened, and sustained not merely by the extrinsic value which they possess as historical documents, but by their intrinsic merits as precious contributions to the literature and philosophy of the world.

E. J. DILLON.

Constantinople,
New Year's Day, 1895.

CONTENTS

	Page
THE POEM OF JOB	1
HEBREW PHILOSOPHY	3
THE PROBLEM OF THE POEM	9
JOB'S METHOD OF SOLVING THE PROBLEM	21
DATE OF THE COMPOSITION	35
THE TEXT AND ITS RECONSTRUCTION	43
INTERPOLATIONS	53
JOB'S THEOLOGICAL AND PHILOSOPHICAL CONCEPTIONS	61
ANALYSIS OF THE POEM	69
KOHELETH	85
CONDITION OF THE TEXT	87
PRIMITIVE FORM OF THE BOOK	91
KOHELETH'S THEORY OF LIFE	99
PRACTICAL WISDOM	105
KOHELETH'S PHILOSOPHY OF LIFE	109
THE SOURCES OF KOHELETH'S PHILOSOPHY	117

CONTENTS

AGUR THE AGNOSTIC 131

AGUR, SON OF YAKEH . . 133
FORM AND CONTENTS OF THE SAYINGS OF AGUR 137
DATE OF COMPOSITION 147
AGUR'S PHILOSOPHY . 151

THE POEM OF JOB (TRANSLATION OF THE RESTORED TEXT) 157

THE SPEAKER (TRANSLATION OF THE RESTORED TEXT) 239

THE SAYINGS OF AGUR (TRANSLATION OF THE RESTORED TEXT) 267

INDEX 273

THE POEM OF JOB

A

HEBREW PHILOSOPHY

According to a theory which was still in vogue a few years ago, the ancient races of mankind were distinguished from each other no less by their intellectual equipment than by their physical peculiarities. Thus the Semites were supposed to be characterised, among other things, by an inborn aptitude for historical narrative and an utter lack of the mental suppleness, ingenuity, and sharp incisive vision indispensable for the study of the problems of philosophy; while their neighbours, the Aryans, devoid of historical talent, were held to be richly endowed with all the essential qualities of mind needed for the cultivation of epic poetry and abstruse metaphysics. This theory has since been abandoned, and many of the alleged facts that once seemed to support it have been shown to be unwarranted assumptions. Thus, the conclusive proof, supplied by Biblical criticism, of the untrustworthiness of the historical books of the Old Testament, has removed one alleged difference between Aryans and Semites, while the discoveries which led to the reconstruction of the primitive poem of Job and of the treatise of Koheleth have undermined the basis of the other. For these two works deal exclusively with philosophical problems, and, together with the Books of Proverbs and Jesus Sirach, are the only remains that have come down to us of the ethical and metaphysical speculations of the ancient Hebrews whose descendants have so materially contributed to further this much-maligned branch of human knowledge. And if we may judge by what we know of these two books, we have ample grounds for regretting that numerous other philosophical treatises which were written between the fourth and the first centuries B.C. were deemed too abstruse, too irrelevant, or too heterodox to find a place in the Jewish Canon.[1] For the Book of Job is an unrivalled masterpiece, the work of one in whom poetry was no mere special faculty cultivated apart from his other gifts, but the outcome of the harmonious wholeness of healthy human nature, in which upright living, untrammelled thought, deep mental vision, and luxuriant imagination combined to form the individual. Hence the poem is a true reflex of the author's mind: it dissolves and blends in harmonious union elements that appeared not merely heterogeneous, but wholly incompatible, and realises, with the concreteness of history, the seemingly unattainable idea which Lucretius had the mind to conceive but lacked the artistic hand to execute; in a word, it is the fruit of the intimate union of that philosophy which, reckless of results,

---

[1] Job and Ecclesiastes were inserted in the Jewish and, one may add, the Christian Canon, solely on the strength of passages which the authors of these compositions never even saw, and which flatly contradict the main theses of their works.

dares to clip even angels' wings, and of the art which possesses the secret of painting its unfading pictures with the delicate tints of the rainbow. Rich fancy and profound thought co-operate to produce a *tertium quid* —a visible proof that the beautiful is one with the true —for which neither literature nor philosophy possesses a name. It is no wonder, then, that this unique poem, which gives adequate utterance to abstract thought, truly and forcibly states the doubts and misgivings which harrow the souls of thinking men of all ages and nations, and helps them to lift a corner of the veil of delusion and get a glimpse of the darkness of the everlasting Night beyond, should appeal to the reader of the nineteenth century with much greater force than to the Jews of olden times, who were accustomed to gauge the sublimity of imaginative poetry and the depth of philosophic speculation by the standard of orthodoxy and the bias of nationality.

The Book of Job, from which Pope Gregory the Great fancied he could piece together the entire system of Catholic theology, and which Thomas of Aquin regarded as a sober history, is now known to be a regular poem, but, as Tennyson truly remarked, "the greatest poem whether of ancient or modern times," and the diction of which even Luther instinctively felt to be "magnificent and sublime as no other book of Scripture." And it is exclusively in this light, as one of the masterpieces of the world's literature, that it will be considered in the following pages. Whatever religious significance it may be supposed to possess over and above, as one of the canonical books of the

Hebrew and Christian Scriptures, will, it is hoped, remain unaffected by this treatment, which is least of all controversial. The flowers that yield honey to the bee likewise delight the bee-keeper with their perfume and the poet with their colours, and there is no adequate reason why the magic verse which strikes a responsive chord in the soul of lovers of high art, and starts a new train of ideas in the minds of serious thinkers, should thereby lose any of the healing virtues it may have heretofore possessed for the suffering souls of the believing.

But viewed even as a mere work of art, it would be hopeless to endeavour to press it into the frame of any one of the received categories of literary composition, as is evident from the fact that authorised and un-authorised opinion on the subject has touched every extreme, and still continues oscillating to-day. Many commentators still treat it as a curious chapter of old-world history narrated with scrupulous fidelity by the hero or an eye-witness, others as a philosophical dialogue; several scholars regard it as a genuine drama, while not a few enthusiastically aver that it is the only epic poem ever written by a Hebrew. In truth, it partakes of the nature of each and every one of these categories, and is yet circumscribed by the laws and limits of none of them. In form, it is most nearly akin to the drama, with which we should be disposed to identify it if the characters of the prologue and epilogue were introduced as *dramatis personæ* in action. But their doing and enduring are presupposed as accomplished facts, and employed merely as a foil to the dialogues, which alone are the work of the author. Perhaps the least erroneous way succinctly to describe what in fact is a *unicum* would be to call it a psychological drama.

Koheleth, or the Preacher, is likewise a literary puzzle which for centuries has baffled the efforts of commentators and aroused the misgivings of theologians. Regarded by many as a *vade mecum* of materialists, by some as an eloquent sermon on the fear of God, and by others as a summary of sceptical philosophy, it is impossible to analyse and classify it without having first eliminated all those numerous later-date insertions which, without improving the author's theology, utterly obscure his meaning and entirely spoil his work. When, by the aid of text criticism, we have succeeded in weeding it of the parasitic growth of ages, we have still to allow for the changing of places of numerous authentic passages either by accident or design, the effects of which are oftentimes quite as misleading as those of the deliberate interpolations. The work thus restored, although one, coherent and logical, is still susceptible of various interpretations, according to the point of view of the reader, none of which, however, can ignore the significant fact that the sceptically ideal basis of Koheleth's metaphysics is identical with that of Buddha, Kant, and Schopenhauer, and admirably harmonises with the ethics of Job and the pessimism of the New Testament.

The Sayings of Agur, on the contrary, tell their own interesting story, without need of note or commentary, to him who possesses a fair knowledge of Hebrew grammar, and an average allowance of mother wit. The lively versifier, the keenness of whose sense of humour is excelled only by the bitterness of his satire, could ill afford to be obscure. A member of the literary fraternity which boasts the names of Lucian and Voltaire, a firm believer in the force of common sense and rudimentary logic, Agur ridicules the theologians of his day with a malicious cruelty which is explained, if not warranted, by the pretensions of omniscience and the practice of intolerance that provoked it. The unanswerable argument which Jahveh considered sufficient to silence his servant Job, Agur deems effective against the dogmatical doctors of his own day:

> "Who has ascended into heaven and come down again?
>
> *   *   *   *   *
>
> Such an one would I question about God: What is his name?"

THE PROBLEM OF THE POEM

Purged of all later interpolations and restored as far as possible to the form it received from the hand of its author, the poem of Job is the most striking presentation of the most obscure and fascinating problem that ever puzzled and tortured the human intellect: how to reconcile the existence of evil, not merely with the fundamental dogmas of the ancient Jewish faith, but with any form of Theism whatever. Stated in the terms in which the poet—whom for convenience sake we shall identify with his hero[1]—manifestly conceived it, it is this: Can God be the creator of all things and yet not be responsible for evil?

The Infinite Being who laid the earth's foundation, "shut in the sea with doors," whose voice is thunder and whose creatures are all things that have being, is, we trust, moral and good. But it is His omnipotence that strikes us most forcibly. Almighty in theory, He is all active in fact, and nothing that happens in the universe is brought about even indirectly by any one but Himself. There are no second causes at work, no chance, no laws of nature, no subordinate agents, nothing that is not the immediate manifestation of His

---

[1] Although the former was a Jew and the latter a Gentile.

free will.[1] This is evident to our senses. But what is equally obvious is that His acts do not tally with His attribute of goodness, and that no facts known or imaginable can help us to bridge over the abyss between the infinite justice ascribed to Him and the crying wrongs that confront us in His universe, whithersoever we turn.[2] His rule is such a congeries of evils that even the just man often welcomes death as a release, and Job himself with difficulty overcame the temptation to end his sufferings by suicide. All the cut-and-dried explanations of God's conduct offered by His human advocates merely render the problem more complicated. His professional apologists are "weavers of lies," and contend for Him "with deception," and, worse than all else, He Himself has never revealed to His creatures any truth more soothing than the fact they set out with, that the problem is for ever insoluble. Wisdom "is hid from the eyes of all living,"[3]

---

[1] *Cf.* Translation, strophe ci. :
  "Is not the soul of every living thing in his hand,
  And the breath of all mankind?"
Strophe civ. :
  "With him is strength and wisdom,
  The erring one and his error are his."
[2] Strophe cxcii.–cxciii. :
  "Look upon me and tremble,
  And lay your hand upon your mouth!
  When I remember I am dismayed,
  And trembling taketh hold on my flesh."
Strophe ccxxi. :
  "Why do the times of judgment depend upon the Almighty,
  And yet they who know him do not see his days?"
[3] Strophe ccxxxiv.

and the dead are in "the land of darkness and of gloom,"[1] whence there is no issue.

The theological views prevalent in the days of the poet, as expounded by the three friends of Job, instead of suggesting some way out of the difficulty were in flagrant contradiction with fact. They appealed to the traditional theory and insisted on having that accepted as the reality. And it was one of the saddest theories ever invented. Virtue was at best a mere matter of business, one of the crudest forms of utilitarianism, a bargain between Jahveh and His creatures. As asceticism in ancient India was rewarded with the spiritual gift of working miracles, so upright living was followed in Judea by material wealth, prosperity, a numerous progeny and all the good things that seem to make life worth living. Such at least was the theory, and those who were satisfied with their lot had little temptation to find fault with it for the sake of those who were not. In sober reality, however, the obligation was very one-sided: Jahveh, who occasionally failed to carry out His threats, observed or repudiated His solemn promises as He thought fit, whereas those among His creatures who faithfully fulfilled their part of the contract were never sure of receiving their stipulated wage in the promised coin. And at that time none other was current: there was no future life looming in the dim distance with intensified rewards and punishments wherewith to redress the balance of this. And it sadly needed redressing. The victims of

---

[1] Strophe lxxxix.

seeming injustice naturally felt that they were being hardly dealt with. And as if to make confusion worse confounded, their neighbours, who had ridden roughshod over all law, human and divine, were frequently exempt from misfortune, lived on the fat of the land, and enjoyed a monopoly of the divine blessings. To Job, whose consciousness of his own righteousness was clearer and less questionable than the justice of his Creator, this theory of retribution seemed unworthy of belief.

The creation of this good God, then, is largely leavened with evil for which—all things being the work of His hands—He, and He alone, is answerable. There was no devil in those olden times upon whose broad shoulders the responsibility for sickness, suffering, misery and death could be conveniently shifted. The Satan or Adversary is still one of the sons of God who, like all his brethren, has free access to the council chamber of the Most High, where he is wont to take a critical, somewhat cynical but not wholly incorrect view of motives and of men. In the government of the world he has neither hand nor part, and his interference in the affairs of Job is the result of a special permission accorded him by the Creator. God alone is the author of good *and of evil*,[1] and the thesis to be demonstrated by His professional apologists consists in showing that the former is the outflow of His mercy, and the latter the necessary effect of His justice acting upon the depraved will of His

---

[1] "The erring one and his error are his" (God's): strophe civ. *Cf.* also strophe cvii.

creatures. But the proof was not forthcoming. Personal suffering might reasonably be explained in many cases as the meet and inevitable wage for wrong-doing; but assuredly not in all. Job himself was a striking instance of unmerited punishment. Even Jahveh solemnly declares him to be just and perfect; and Job was admittedly no solitary exception; he was the type of a numerous class of righteous, wronged and wretched mortals, unnamed and unknown:

> "Omnes illacrymabiles ....
>   ignotique longa
> Nocte, carent quia vate sacro."

Job is ready to admit that God, no doubt, is just and good in theory, but he cannot dissemble the obvious fact that His works in the universe are neither; indeed, if we may judge the tree by its fruits, His *régime* is the rule of an oriental and almighty despot whose will and pleasure is the sole moral law. And that will is too often undistinguishable from malice of the blackest kind. Thus

> "He destroyeth the upright and the wicked,
> When his scourge slayeth at unawares.
> He scoffeth at the trial of the innocent;
> The earth is given into the hand of the wicked."

In a word, the poet proclaims that the current theories of traditional theology were disembodied, not incarnate in the moral order of the world, had, in fact, nowhere taken root.

The two most specious arguments with which it was sought to prop up this tottering theological system consisted in maintaining that the wicked are often punished and the good recompensed in their offspring —a kind of spiritual entail in which the tenant for life is denied the usufruct for the sake of heirs he never knew—and that such individual claims as were left unadjusted by this curious arrangement were merged in those of the community at large and should be held to be settled in full as long as the weal of the nation was assured. In other words, the individual sows and his offspring or the nation reaps the harvest. But Job rejects both pleas as illusory and immoral, besides which, they leave the frequent prosperity of the unrighteous unexplained. "Wherefore," he asks, "do the wicked live, become old, yea wax mighty in strength?" The reply that the fathers having eaten sour grapes, the children's teeth will be set on edge, is, he contends, no answer to the objection; it merely intensifies it. For he who sows should reap, and he who sins should suffer. After death the most terrible punishment meted out to the posterity of criminals is powerless to affect their mouldering dust. That, surely, cannot be accepted as a vindication of justice, human or divine.

> "Ye say: God hoards punishment for the children.
>   Let him rather requite the wicked himself that he may feel it!
>   His own eyes should behold his downfall,
>   And he himself should drain the Almighty's wrath.
>   If his sons are honoured, he will not know it;
>   And if dishonoured, he will not perceive it.
>   Only in his own flesh doth he feel pain,
>   And for his own soul will he lament."

As to the latter argument, that the well-being of the nation was a settlement in full of the individual's claims to happiness, it was equally irrelevant, even had the principle underlying it been confirmed by experience. Granting that a certain wholesale kind of equity was administered, why must the individual suffer for no fault of his own? Wherein lies the justice of a Being who, credited with omnipotence, permits that by a sweep of the wild hurricane of disaster, "green leaves with yellow mixed are torn away"?

But the contention that, viewing the individual merely as a unit of the aggregate, justice would be found to be dealt out fairly on the whole, ran counter to experience. The facts were dead against it. The Hebrew nation had fared as badly among neighbouring states as Job among his friends and countrymen. In this respect the sorely tried individual was the type of his nation. The destruction of the kingdom of Samaria which had occurred nearly two hundred years before and the captivity of Judah, which was not yet at an end, gave its death-blow to the theory. "The tents of robbers prosper and they that provoke Shaddai[1] are secure."

In truth, there was but one issue out of the difficulty: divine justice might not be bounded by time or space; the law of compensation might have a larger field than our earth for its arena; a future life might afford "time" and opportunity to right the wrongs of the present, and all end well in the best of future worlds.

---

[1] God.

This explanation would have set doubts at rest and settled the question for at least two thousand years; and it seemed such a necessary postulate to the fathers of the Church, who viewed the matter in the light of Christian revelation, that they actually put into Job's mouth the words which he would have uttered had he lived in their own days and been a member of the true fold. And they effected this with a pious recklessness of artistic results and of elementary logic that speaks better for their intentions than for their æsthetic taste. In truth, Job knows absolutely nothing of a future life, and his friends, equally unenlightened, see nothing for it but to "discourse wickedly for God," and "utter lies on His behalf."[1] There was, in fact, no third course. Indeed, if the hero or his friends had even suspected the possibility of a solution based upon a life beyond the tomb, the problem on which the book is founded would not have existed. To ground, therefore, the doctrines of the Resurrection, the Atonement, &c., upon alleged passages of the poem of Job is tantamount to inferring the squareness of a circle from its perfect rotundity. In the Authorised Version of the Bible the famous verses, which have probably played a more important part in the intellectual history of mankind than all the books of the Old Testament put together, run thus: "For I know *that* my redeemer liveth, and *that* he shall stand at the latter *day* upon the earth: and *though* after my skin *worms* destroy this *body*, yet in my flesh shall I see God: whom I shall see for

---

[1] Strophe cxi.

myself, and mine eyes shall behold, and not another; *though* my reins be consumed within me."[1]

Now this, it is hardly necessary to say, is not a translation from the poem nor from any known text of it, but the embodiment of the salutary beliefs of well-intentioned theologians—of St. Jerome among others—momentarily forgetful of the passage: "Will ye speak wickedly for God?" The Christian conception of a Redeemer would, had he but known it, have proved balm to the heart of the despairing hero. As a matter of mere fact, his own hope at that critical moment was less sublime and very much less Christian: the coming of an avenger who would punish his enemies and rehabilitate his name. It was the one worldly and vain longing that still bound him to the earth. Other people demanded happiness as their reward for virtue, too often undistinguishable from vice; Job challenged the express approval of the Deity, asked only that he should not be confounded with vulgar sinners. The typical perfect man, struck down with a loathsome disease, doomed to a horrible death, alone in his misery, derided by his enemies, and, worse than all, loathed as a common criminal by those near and dear to him, gives his friends and enemies, society and theologians, the lie emphatic—nay, he goes the length of affirming that God Himself has failed in His duty towards him.

---

[1] Job xix. 25-27. The Revised Version gives the passage as follows: "But I know that my redeemer liveth, and that he shall stand up at the last upon the earth: and after my skin hath been thus destroyed, yet from my flesh shall I see God: whom I shall see for myself, and mine eyes shall behold, and not another."

"Know, then, that God hath wronged me."[1] His conscience, however, tells him that inasmuch as there is such a thing as eternal justice, a time will come when the truth will be proclaimed and his honour fully vindicated; Shaddai will then yearn for the work of His hands, but it will be too late, "For now I must lay myself down in the dust; and Thou shalt seek me, but I shall not be." And it is to this conviction, not to a belief in future retribution, that the hero gives utterance in the memorable passage in question:

> "But I know that my avenger liveth,
> Though it be at the end upon my dust;
> My witness will avenge these things,
> And a curse alight upon mine enemies."

He knows nothing whatever of the subsistence of our cumbrous clods of clay after they have become the food of worms and pismires; indeed, he is absolutely certain that by the sleep of death

> "we end
> The heartache, and the thousand natural shocks
> That flesh is heir to."

And he emphasises his views in a way that should have given food for wholesome reflection to his commentators.

> "There is a future for the tree,
> And hope remaineth to the palm;
> Cut down, it will sprout again,
> And its tender branch will not cease.

---

[1] Strophe clxix.

"Though its roots wax old in the earth,
 And its stock lie buried in mould,
 Yet through vapour of water will it bud,
 And put forth boughs like a plant.

"But man dieth and lieth outstretched;
 He giveth up the ghost, where is he then?
 He lieth down and riseth not up;
 Till heaven be no more he shall not awake."[1]

Nothing could well be further removed from the comforting hope of a future life, the resurrection of the body, and eternal rewards, than this unshaken belief that Death is our sole redeemer from the terrible evils of life.

---

[1] Job, strophes cxxiv.–cxxvi. of my English translation.

JOB'S METHOD OF SOLVING THE PROBLEM

It is perhaps hardly necessary to point out that the doctrine of eternal pains and rewards as laid down by the Christian Church, unless reinforced by faith, neither solves the problem nor simplifies it. If the truth must be told, it seems to unenlightened reason to entangle it more hopelessly than before. In simple terms and in its broadest aspect the question may be stated as follows: God created man under conditions of His own choosing which necessarily led to the life-long misery of countless millions upon earth and their never-ending torments in hell. To the question, Did He know the inevitable effect of His creative act, the answer is, God is omniscient. To the query, Could He have selected other and more humane conditions of existence for His creature—conditions so adjusted that, either with or without probation, man would have been ultimately happy? the reply is, God is almighty.

Involuntarily, then, the question forces itself upon us, Is He all-good? Can that Being be deemed good who, moved by no necessity, free to create or to abstain from creating, at liberty to create for happiness or for misery, calls mankind into existence under such conditions and surroundings that myriads are miserable, so unutterably miserable, that, compared with their tortures, the wretch bleeding and quivering on the wheel is lolling in the lap of enjoyment? Why did God make man under such conditions? Or at least how are we to reconcile His having done so with His attribute of goodness? To this question there are many replies but no answer, the former being merely attempts to explain the chronic effects of the primordial ethical poison commonly called original sin.

Job's main objection to the theological theories in vogue among his contemporaries, and, indeed, to all conceivable explanations of the difficulty, is far more weighty than at first sight appears. Everything, he tells us—if anything—is the work of God's hands; and as pain, suffering, evil, are everywhere predominant, it is not easy to understand in what sense God can be said to be good. The poet does not formulate the argument, of which this is the gist, in very precise terms, nor press it home to its last conclusions. But he leaves no doubt about his meaning. Some men are relatively good by nature, others wicked; but all men were created by God and act in accordance with the disposition they received from Him. If that disposition or character brought forth sin and evil, these then are God's work, not man's, and He alone is responsible therefor. The individual who performs an act through an agent is rightly deemed to have done it himself. A man, therefore, who, being free to do a certain thing or to leave it undone, and perfectly aware of the nature of its necessary consequences, performs it, is held to be answerable for the results, should they prove mischievous. Much greater is his responsibility if, instead of being restricted to the choice between undertaking a work certain to prove pernicious and abstaining from it, he was free to select a third course and to accomplish it in such a way that the result would not be evil, but unmixed good. In this case it would hardly seem possible to exonerate the doer from a charge of wanton malice, diabolic in degree. And such is the position in which many theologians seem—to those who view things in the light of reason—to have placed God Himself. It was open to Him, they maintain, to create or to refrain from creating. Having declared for the former alternative, He is chargeable with the consequences. The consequences, however, need not have been evil; He might, had He so willed it, have endowed His creature with such qualities and placed him in such surroundings that, without ceasing to be man, he would never have fallen at all. Yet it did not please Him to adopt that course. This admission, rationalists urge, is conclusive as to the origin of sin and evil.

But the arguments are not yet exhausted. Even then the Creator might have made everything right by an act which it seems impossible to distinguish from elementary justice. Had He regarded the first man who brought sin into the world as a mere individual, and treated him as such—and this, theologians assure us, He could easily have done[1]—He might have pun-

---

[1] One of the best accredited exponents of this theory, which is

ished him as an individual, and the matter would have been at an end. But instead of this, He contemplated him as the type and representative of the human race, and decreed that his sin should, like a subtle spiritual poison, infect the soul of every man coming into the world. In other words, God, who is supposed to hate evil so profoundly that He damns for ever in hell a man guilty of one single "mortal" transgression, enacted that if one sin were committed it should be needlessly made to engender myriads of other sins, and that the tiny seed of evil which was first thrown upon the earth by His creature in a moment of pardonable weakness, and might have so easily been trampled out, should take root, sprout up and grow into a vast Upas tree whose poisonous branches overshadow all creation. This proposition, it is contended, explicitly taxes God, if not with the sole authorship of sin and evil, at least with the moral responsibility for propagating it. And this is the prevailing view among modern apologists.

As to the origin of evil, it is to be sought for, theologians have discovered, in the free will with which God endowed man. This, they allege, shifts all the responsibility on the human creature because, instead of evil, he might have chosen good. Unfortunately, the same argument would seem to apply to the Creator Himself.[1] He, too, being omnipotent, might have chosen good instead of evil subjects, and created human beings whose acts would have been blameless and virtuous,

---

now generally accepted by Catholic divines, is Father (now Cardinal) Mazella.

[1] And Job more than once applies it.

their will remaining what it is. Further, not having done this and having needlessly allowed an abyss to be made by sin between Himself and the first man, it was still open to Him to have abstained from widening it until it became an impassable gulf between Himself and the entire human race. But He did not abstain; instead of localising, He deliberately and wantonly spread the evil, and the ruin that overwhelmed all mankind cannot therefore be said to have sprung from the will of the race, but from His own. Again, the interposition of a free will between God and evil, it is urged, affords no real solution of the problem, for the question still remains, why were the workings of that free will evil and not good? Obviously because such was its God-created nature; for the action of outward circumstances upon the will neither builds up nor modifies this nature, but simply discloses it to our view.

These ideas were adopted, developed and defended by a few of the most profound Christian philosophers of the early Church, and most ably of all by Scotus Erigena,[1] who held that the origin of evil which cannot be sought for in God must not be placed *in the free will of man,* because the latter hypothesis would still leave the responsibility with the Creator, the human will being His own handiwork.

At the root of this argument lies yet another consideration upon which unbelieving thinkers rely still more: it is drawn from the alleged incompatibility between the conception of a created being and free

---

[1] *Cf.* Editio Princeps, Oxford, 1681, p. 287.

will, and will be noticed presently. It is commonly regarded as the principal difficulty which Theists and Pantheists are condemned continually to encounter without ever being able to explain—the rock, so to say, upon which their optimistic systems strike, and are shattered to pieces—unless protected by the armour of supernatural faith.

But besides the Christian and Pantheistic theories, there is another explanation of the origin of evil offered by the religion of more than one-third of the human race. It is a theory which can readily be labelled and libelled by the most unphilosophical reader, but cannot be grasped and appreciated without serious study and reflection by the most intelligent, for it is based upon the doctrine that time, space and causality have no existence outside the human mind.[1] The world which we see and know, therefore, and everything it contains is " such stuff as dreams are made of "—the woof and warp being evolved from, and interwoven by, our own minds. Underlying the innumerable illusive appearances which we call the world is a reality, a being or force which is one. We and everything else

---

[1] Many pious Christians who scoff at such notions, without endeavouring to understand them, would do well to remember that whatever truth there is in the dogma of the immortality of the soul, is dependent upon this proposition, that time, space, and the law of causality have no real existence whatever, but are merely the furniture of the human mind—the forms in which it apprehends. As time exists only in our consciousness, and as beginning and end can take place only in time, they can affect only our consciousness, which ends in death, but not our souls, which are distinct from mind and consciousness.

are but manifestations, in time and space, of this one reality with which, however, each and every one of us is at bottom identical and whose sole attribute is unity. This force or will manifests itself in myriads of facets, so to say, in the universe, and these manifestations are not good, constitute, indeed, a sort of fall. Intelligence is not one of the primary attributes of this eternal will. It attained to clear consciousness and knowledge only in man and then for the first time perceived that the existence for which it yearned is evil and not good. Man therefore is his own work; and existence, as it constitutes a fall, is its own punishment; for his life is a series of inane desires which, when momentarily satiated, are immediately succeeded by others equally vain, fruitless and hollow, and the cessation of desire is the beginning of tedium which is oftentimes still less endurable, seeing that it leaves little room for hope.

> " Life which ye prize is long-drawn agony;
> Only its pains abide, its pleasures are
> As birds which light and fly."

Every wish springs from want which causes pain, the attainment of the wished-for object—commonly called pleasure—is but the cessation of that pain: in other words it is a mere negation. Man's life is a never-ending oscillation between pleasure and pain: the former mere illusion, the latter a dread reality. The origin of this and of all other evil is individual existence, and individual existence is the free act of the one substance or force which is identical with each and all of us.

This theory excludes creation. For free will is utterly incompatible with the state of a created being;[1] because *operari sequitur esse*—*i.e.*, the operation, the working of every being, must be the necessary result of its qualities which are themselves known only by the acts they bring forth. If these acts be praiseworthy, the qualities are good: if reprehensible, they are bad. But if the acts are to be free, they should be neither good nor bad. A being therefore to be perfectly free should have no qualities at all—*i.e.*, should not be created. For it must be borne in mind that it is not the motives that impart to the will its ethical quality. Motives are accidental and operate in the same way as the rays of the sun falling upon a tree or a flower: they reveal the nature of the object but are powerless to change it, for better or for worse.[2] But if this be so, one may ask, why do we feel sorrow, shame, repentance for acts which we were not free to perform or abstain from performing? Because we are "metaphysically" free, that is to say, our inborn disposition from which they necessarily emanate, is the work of our free will, which specific acts are not. No doubt, when we do right or wrong, we are conscious that we might have acted differently—*had we willed it*. But this proves nothing; the all-important question being, could we, under the circumstances, have willed otherwise than we did? And to this the reply is an em-

---

[1] Job, who rejected all secondary causes whatever, could not in logic, and did not in fact, believe in free will as it is commonly understood in our days.

[2] *Cf.* Matt. xii. 33-35.

phatic negative. But for our personal character, be it good or evil, we are answerable, and therefore likewise for the acts that flow from it with the rigorous necessity characteristic of all causality. For individuality in the human race is identical with character, and as individuality is the work of our own free will exercised outside the realm of time and space, we are responsible for it, and conscious of the responsibility, although not of the manner in which it was incurred.

Our acts, therefore, and they only, show us what we really are; our sufferings what we deserve. The former are the necessary outcome of our character which external circumstances, in the guise of motives, call into play; just as gravitation is acted upon when we shake an apple off the tree. Our deeds then being the inevitable resultant of that self-created character acted upon by motives, must consequently follow with the same necessity as any other link in the chain of cause and effect. The knowledge of our character and the foreknowledge of these outward events which, in the unbroken chain of cause and effect, act upon it, would suffice to enable us to foresee our future as readily as astronomers foresee eclipses of the sun and moon. Now if the root of all evil be individuality, the essence of all morality is self-denial; and no act performed for the purpose of obtaining happiness, temporal or eternal, is moral. The evil and pain, therefore, which befall us upon earth cannot be regarded as the retribution for the deeds done in this life; for these are necessary and inevitable. They are the fruits of our character whence these acts emanate; and it is only our character which is our own work. With the ethical nature of that character each individual gradually grows acquainted as well in his own case as in that of his neighbour's, solely from a study of his own acts, which often astonish himself quite as much as his friends.

Brahmanism and Buddhism symbolized these notions in the somewhat gross but only intelligible form in which the mind can readily grasp them, viz., in the dogma of the transmigration of souls, according to which a man's good deeds and bad follow him like his shadow from one existence to another, and in this life he expiates the sins or enjoys the fruits of a previous existence:[1]

> " Each man's life
> The outcome of his former living is;
> The bygone wrongs bring forth sorrows and woes,
> The bygone right breeds bliss.
>
> " That which ye sow ye reap. See yonder fields!
> The sesamum was sesamum, the corn
> Was corn. The Silence and the Darkness knew!
> So is man's fate born."

Even the Bible is not wholly devoid of traces of the same symbol employed to convey the same ideas; cf. Matt. xi. 14, John ix. 2, for the New Testament, and Ps. xc. 3 for the Old. The apparent inner absurdity of the doctrine of the transmigration of souls arises mainly from our inability to grasp and realise the two propositions which it presupposes—viz., that there is no such thing as time outside of the human mind, and therefore no past or future; and, secondly, that soul is but individualised will momentarily illumined by the intellect which is a function of the brain. Metempsychosis was originally no more than a symbol.

In the former religion, Brahma, who is identical with all of us, produces the world by a kind of fall from his primeval state and remains therein until he has redeemed himself. In the latter there is no god; man being his own handiwork and sin and evil the result of his blind striving after individual existence. It is however in his power, and in his alone, to right the wrong and remedy the evil, by starving out the fatal hunger for life. And in this work, faith, supplication and sacrifice avail him nothing.

> "Pray not! the Darkness will not brighten! Ask
> Nought from the Silence, for it cannot speak!
> Vex not your mournful minds with pious pains!
> Ah, brothers, sisters! seek
> Naught from the helpless gods by gift and hymn,
> Nor bribe with blood, nor feed with fruits and cake;
> Within yourself deliverance must be sought:
> Each man his prison makes."

The ethical bearing of this view is more easily discerned than its metaphysical basis. Individual existence with its tantalising mirage of pleasures being the root of all evil, the first step towards finding a remedy is to recognise this truth, to obtain insight into the heart of things athwart the veil of Maya or delusion. The conviction that all beings are not merely brothers but one and the same essence, is the death of egotistic desire, of the pernicious distinction between me and thee, and the birth of pity, love and sympathy for all men. And this is a very old doctrine. In India it was taught in the Veda and the Vedanta under the formula *tat tvam asi*

—thou art this—*i.e.*, individual differs not essentially from individual, nor a man from the whole human race. He who obtains this insight and perceives how sorrow is shadow to life, who weans his thirst for existence, seeks not, strives not, wrongs not, starves out his passions, resigns himself wholly to pain and suffering as to "ills that flow from foregone wrongfulness" and asks for no clue from the Silence which can utter naught, he is truly blessed and released from all misery forever. He glides "lifeless to nameless quiet, nameless joy, blessed Nirvāna."

It is probable, not to say certain, that it was an intuition of this kind that finally reconciled Job with the grey monotony of misery and seeming injustice which characterises all human existence and enabled him to resign himself cheerfully to whatever might befall. This at least would seem to be the only reasonable construction of which Jahveh's apparition and discourse are susceptible. That they are resorted to by the poet solely as an image and symbol of the inner illumination of his hero's intellect, is evident to most readers. Nothing that Jahveh has to disclose to Job and his three friends even remotely resembles a clue to the problem that exercised them. The human mind would be unable to grasp a solution if any existed, for it possesses no forms in which to apprehend it. This will soon become apparent even to the non-philosophical reader who endeavours to *reason* about a state in which time, space, *and causality* have no existence. But there is no solution. Jahveh virtually asks, as Buddha had asked before:

> "Shall any gazer see with mortal eyes,
> Or any searcher know with mortal mind?
> Veil after veil will lift—but there must be
> Veil upon veil behind."

Unless we assume some such sudden illumination of the mind as Buddha obtained under the shadow of the fig-tree and the author of the 73rd Psalm among the ruins of the kingdom of Juda, it is impossible to account for Job's unforeseen and entire resignation, or to bring his former defiant utterances into harmony with the humble sentiments to which he now gives expression. For nothing but his mind had meanwhile undergone a change. All the elements of the problem remained what they were. The evils that had fired his indignation were not denied by their presumptive author, nor was any explanation of them vouchsafed to him. No remedy was promised in this life, no hope held out of redress in a possible world to come. On the contrary, Jahveh confirms the terrible facts alleged by His servant; He admits that pleasure and pain are not the meed of deeds done upon earth, and that the explanation we seek, the light we so wistfully long for, will never come; for human existence is not a dark spot in an ocean of dazzling splendour, but a will'-o'-the-wisp that merely intensifies the murkiness of everlasting Night.

Moreover, Job was detached from the world already. He had overcome all his passions and kept even his legitimate affections under control. He had no word of regret on losing his cattle, his possessions, his children. During his most exquisite sufferings, he declared that he held only to his good name. This, too, he now gives up and demanding nothing, avers that he is satisfied. "I resign and console myself. Though it be in dust and ashes." Complete detachment from existence, and not for the sake of some other and better existence (for there is none) is the practical outcome of Job's intuition. But in a God-created world made for the delectation of mankind, to forego its pleasures would be to offend the Creator, if indeed stark madness could kindle His ire. But to curb one's thirst for life and to spurn its joys because one holds them to be the tap root of all evil, is an action at once intelligible and wise. And this is what Job evidently does when he practises difficult virtues and undergoes terrible sufferings without the consciousness of past guilt or the faintest hope of future recompense.

As Buddha taught his followers: "When the disciple has lost all doubt as to the reality of suffering; when his doubts as to the origin of suffering are dispelled; when he is no longer uncertain as to the possibility of annihilating suffering and when he hesitates no more about the way that leads to the annihilation of suffering: then is he called a holy disciple, one who is in the stream that floweth onwards to perfection, one who is delivered from evil, who is guaranteed, who is devoted to the highest truth."[1]

---

[1] "Samyuttaka-Nikāyo," vol. iii. chap. iii. p. 24. *Cf.* Dr. K. E. Neumann's "Buddhistische Anthologie," Leiden, 1892, p. 204.

DATE OF THE COMPOSITION

THE question which frequently exercised the ingenuity of former commentators, whether the poem of Job is the work of one or of many authors, has no longer any actuality. It is absolutely certain that the book, as we find it in the Authorised Version, and even in the best Hebrew manuscripts, is a mosaic put together by a number of writers widely differing in their theological views and separated from each other by whole centuries; and it is equally undoubted that, restored to its original form, it is "a poem round and perfect as a star"—the masterpiece of one of the most gifted artists of his own or any age. To the inquiry where he lived and wrote, numerous tentative replies have been offered but no final answer. To many he is the last of the venerable race of patriarchs, and his verse the sweet, sublime lisping of a childlike nature, disporting itself in the glorious morning of the world.[1]

---

[1] One of the main grounds for this opinion is the absolute ignorance of the Mosaic law manifested by the author of Job. The line of reasoning is that he must have been either a Jew—and in that case have lived before or simultaneously with Moses—or else an Arab, like his hero, and have written the work in Arabic, Moses himself probably doing it into Hebrew. To a Hebrew scholar this

This, however, is but a pretty fancy, which will not stand the ordeal of scientific criticism, nor even the test of a careful common-sense examination. The broader problems that interest thinking minds of a late and reflective age, the profounder feelings and more ambitious aspirations of manhood and maturity, are writ large in every verse of the poem. The lyre gives out true, full notes, which there is no mistaking. The hero is evidently a travelled cosmopolitan, who has outgrown the narrow prejudices of petty patriotism and national religious creeds to such an extent that he studiously eschews the use of the revealed name of the God of his people, and seems to believe at most in a far-away and incomprehensible divinity who sometimes merges into Fate. In the God of theologians he had no faith. His comforters, who from the uttermost ends of the earth meet together in a most unpatriarchal manner to discuss the higher problems of philosophy, allude to the views in vogue in the patriarchal age as to traditions of bygone days before the influence of foreign invaders had tainted the purity of the national faith; and passages like xii. 17, xv. 19, seem to point to the captivity of the Hebrew people

---

sounds as plausible as would the thesis, to one well versed in Greek, that the Iliad is but a translation from the Sanscrit. The Talmud makes Job now a contemporary of David and Solomon, now wholly denies his existence. Jerome, and some Roman Catholic theologians of to-day, identify the author of the poem with Moses himself, a view in favour of which not a shred of argument can be adduced. *Cf.* Loisy, "Le Livre de Job," Paris, 1892, p. 37; Reuss, "Hiob.," Braunschweig, 1888, pp. 8 ff.

as an accomplished fact. In a word, the strict monotheism of the hero, which at times borders upon half-disguised secularism, has nothing in common with the worship of the patriarchs except the absence of priests and the lack of ceremonies. The language of the poem, flavoured by a strong mixture of Arabic and Aramaic words and phrases, and the frequent use of imagery borrowed from Babylonian mythology, to say nothing of a number of other signs and tokens of a comparatively late age, render the patriarchal hypothesis absolutely untenable.[1] This, at least, is one of the few results of modern research about which there is perfect unanimity among all competent scholars.

If the date of the composition of Job cannot be fixed with any approach to accuracy, there are at least certain broad limits within which it is agreed on all hands that it should be placed. This period is comprised between the prophetic activity of Jeremiah and the second half of the Babylonian Exile. The considerations upon which this opinion is grounded are drawn mainly, if not exclusively, from authentic passages of Job which the author presumably borrowed from other books of the Old Testament. Thus a comparison of the verses in which the hero curses the day of his birth [2] with an identical malediction in Jeremiah (xx. 14-15), and of

---

[1] The subject of the date and place of composition has been treated by Cornill, "Einleitung in das Alte Testament," 235 fol., by Prof. Duhm, "The Book of Job" (*cf.* "The New World," June, 1894), and others. But the most lucid, masterly, and dispassionate discussion of the subject is to be found in Prof. Cheyne's "Job and Solomon," chaps. viii.-xii.   [2] Job A.V. iii. 3-10.

the respective circumstances in which each was written, leads to the conviction that the borrower was not the prophet whose writings must therefore have been familiar to the poet. This conclusion is confirmed by a somewhat far-fetched but none the less valid argument drawn from the circumstance that Ezckiel,[1] who would probably have known the poem had it existed in his day, obviously never heard of it; for this prophet, broaching the question, apparently for the first time among his countrymen, as to the justice of human suffering, denies point blank that any man endures unmerited pain,[2] and affirms in emphatic terms that to each one shall be meted out reward or punishment according to his works.[3] And this he could hardly have done had he been aware of the fact that the contradictory proposition was vouched for by no less an authority than Jahveh Himself.

Again, it is highly probable, although one would hardly be justified in stating it as an established fact, that certain striking poetic images clothed in the same form of words in Job and in the Second Isaiah,[4] are the coinage of the rich imagination of the latter,[5] from

---

[1] 592–572 B.C. [2] Ezek. xviii. 2, 3. [3] *Ibid.* 4–9.

[4] "The Second Isaiah" is the name now usually given to the unknown author of one of the sublimest books of the Old Testament, viz., chaps. xl.–lxvi. of the work commonly attributed to Isaiah. It was composed most probably between 546 and 535 B.C.

[5] They may be found by referring to the parallel passages given in the margin of the Authorised Version of Job; for instance, chap. xiv. One example may suffice: In the Second Isaiah, xl 6–8, we read "The Voice said, Cry. And he said, What shall I cry? All flesh is grass, and all the goodliness thereof *is* as the flower of

whose writings they must consequently have been taken by the author of Job. If this assumption be correct, and it is considerably strengthened by collateral evidence, we should have no choice but to assign to the composition of the poem a date later than that of the Second Isaiah who wrote between 546 and 535 B.C. The ingenious and learned German critic, Dr. Cornill, holds it to be no less than two or three hundred years younger still, and bases his opinion principally upon the last verse of the last chapter of the Book of Job, where the expression (Job died) "old and full of days," is, in his opinion, borrowed from the Priests' Code. It is, however, needless to analyse this argument, seeing that the verse in question was wanting in the Septuagint [1] version, and must therefore be held to be a later addition.

Another question, once a sure test of orthodoxy, the discussion of which has become equally superfluous to-day, is to what extent the narrative is based upon historical facts. The second council of Constantinople

---

the field: the grass withereth, the flower fadeth: because the spirit of the Lord bloweth upon it: surely the people *is* grass. The grass withereth, the flower fadeth: but the word of our God shall stand for ever." In Job we find the winged word embodied in the verse 2, chap. xiv. A.V. (strophe cxxi.).

> "Man that is born of a woman,
> Poor in days and rich in trouble;
> He cometh forth as a flower and fadeth,
> He fleeth like a shadow and abideth not."

[1] For the value of the testimony of the Septuagint, *cf.* following chapter.

solemnly condemned Theodore, Bishop of Mopsuestia, one of the most enlightened Fathers of the Church, for having advanced the opinion that the story of Job was a pious fiction and the doctrine it embodies irreconcileable with orthodoxy. It would be rash to say what conclusion a council sitting at the end of the nineteenth century would be likely to arrive at. But it would hardly find fault with the majority of contemporary critics who hold that the prologue and epilogue, which are in prose and contain in outline the popular legend of Job, were anterior to the colloquies between the hero and his friends, bear in fact the same relation to the poem that the mediæval legend of Johan Faustus does to the masterpiece of Goethe. And it was to the popular legend, not to the poem, that Ezekiel alluded in the passage in which he instances Job as the type of the just man. But one must needs be endowed with a strong and child-like faith to accept, in the light of ancient history and modern science, as sober facts the familiar conversation between Jahveh and the Adversary in the council-chamber of heaven, the sudden intervention of the latter in the life of Job, the ease with which he breaks through the chain of causality and bends even the human will to his purpose, the indecent haste with which he overwhelms the just man with a torrent of calamities in the course of one short day, the apparition of Jahveh in a storm-cloud, and many other equally improbable details. Improbability, however, is the main feature of all miracles; and faith need not be dismayed even by the seemingly impossible. In any case where it is hopeless to convince, it is needless to discuss, and if there still be readers to whose appreciation of the poem belief in its historical truth is absolutely indispensable, it would be cruel to seek to spoil or even lessen their enjoyment of one of the most sublime creations known to any literature of the world.

THE TEXT AND ITS RECONSTRUCTION

Our Authorised Version of Job is based upon the text handed down to us in existing Hebrew manuscripts and upon Jerome's Latin translation. None of the manuscripts, the most important of which are those of the Vatican,[1] of Alexandria[2] and of Sinai,[3] go further back than the fourth century A.D. And some of the modifications, made by Jerome in the Latin translation, particularly in chap. xxi. 25-27, into which he introduces the Christian idea of the Resurrection, were not based upon the various readings of the Codices, but inspired by a pious desire to render the work more edifying. As our Hebrew manuscripts are all derived from a single copy which was probably contemporaneous with the reign of the Emperor Hadrian,[4] the words and the corrections of which they reproduce with Chinese scrupulosity, the utmost we can expect from them is to supply us with the text as it existed at that relatively late age.

The comparative indifference that reigned before that

---

[1] Fourth century A.D.   [2] Fifth century A.D.
[3] Fourth century A.D.   [4] A.D. 117-138.

time as to the purity of the text of the most important books of the Canon, and the utter carelessness with which down to the first century of the Christian era the manuscripts of the Hagiographa [1] were treated, render it highly probable that long before the reign of Hadrian the poem of Job had undergone many and serious modifications. The ease with which words written with consonants only, many of which resembled each other, were liable to be interchanged, strengthens this probability; while a detailed study of the various manuscripts and translations transforms it into certainty. The parallel passages alone of almost any of the books of the Old Testament yield a rich harvest of divergences.

But involuntary errors of the copyists are insufficient to explain all the bewildering changes which disfigure many of the books of the Sacred Scriptures. The gradual evolution of the Hebrew religion from virtual polytheism to the strictest monotheism seemed peremptorily to call for a corresponding change in the writings in which the revelation underlying it was enshrined. A later stadium of the evolution—which, of course, was never felt to be such—might naturally cause the free and easy views and lax practices which once were orthodox and universal to assume the odious form of heresy and impiety, and a laudable respect for the author of revelation was held to impose

---

[1] The Hagiographa—or, as the Hebrews term them, *Ketubim*—include Job, Proverbs, the Psalms, the Canticle of Canticles, Ruth, the Lamentations, Koheleth, Esther, Daniel, Ezra Nehemiah, and Chronicles.

the sacred duty of bringing the documentary records of ancient practices into harmony with present theories. This was especially true of the Books of Job and Ecclesiastes, in which not only was the general tone lacking in respect for all that the Jewish community held sacred, but likewise long and eloquent passages directly called in question the truth of revelation and blasphemously criticised the attributes of the Most High.

Gauged by the narrow standards of the Jewish community,[1] some of Job's most sublime outbursts of poetic passion must have seemed as impious to his contemporaries as to the theologians of our own country the "blasphemies" hurled by Byron's Lucifer against the "Everlasting Tyrant." There can be no doubt that it is to the feeling of holy horror which his plain speaking aroused in the minds of the strait-laced Jews of 2400 years ago that we have to ascribe the principal and most disfiguring changes which the poem underwent at the hands of well-meaning censors. It is quite possible even now to point out, by the help of a few disjointed fragments still preserved, the position, and to divine the sense, of certain spiritful and defiant passages which, in the interest of "religion and morals," were remorselessly suppressed, to indicate

---

[1] As distinguished from the pre-exilian people. Before the Captivity the Israelites lived the political life of all independent nations. After the Exile they were but a religious community—a Church. It was for this Church that the "Mosaic" legislation of the Priests' Code was written and the ancient historical records retouched.

others which were split up and transposed, and to distinguish many prolix discourses, feeble or powerful word-pictures and trite commonplaces which were deliberately inserted later on, for the sole purpose of toning down the most audacious piece of rationalistic philosophy which has ever yet been clothed in the music of sublime verse.

The disastrous results of these corrections which were made at various times and by different persons is writ large in the present text of Job as we find it in the Hebrew manuscripts and our Authorised Version, which offer us in many places a jumble of disjointed fragments, incoherent, irrelevant or self-contradictory.

In addition to common sense aided by cautious text criticism which enables us to recognise interpolations, to correct copyists' errors and occasionally even to determine the place and the tendency of expunged passages, the means at our disposal for the restoration of the poem are principally two: The laws of Hebrew poetry (parallelism and metre) on the one hand, and a comparison of the Hebrew text with the ancient Greek translation of the Septuagint,[1] on the other. A judicious use of these helps which are recognised as such even by the most conservative Christians, who condemn without hearing the tried methods and least doubtful conclusions of biblical criticism, enables one to accomplish all that is now possible towards restoring the poem of Job to its original form.

The nature and the laws of Hebrew metre, the

---

[1] Completed probably in the second century B.C.

THE POEM OF JOB

discovery of which is indissolubly associated with the name of Prof. Bickell,[1] are identical with those of Syriac poetry. The unit is the line, the syllables of which are numbered and accentuated, the line most frequent containing seven syllables with iambic rhythm. Accentuated syllables alternate regularly with unaccentuated, whereby the penultimate has the accent; and the poetic accent always coincides with the grammatical, as in Syriac poetry and in the Greek verse of early Christian times, the structure of which was copied from the Syriac. Compare for instance the following:

> Ἡ παρθένος σήμερον
> Τὸν ἐπουράνιον τίκτει,
> Καὶ ἡ γῆ τὸ σπήλαιον
> Τῷ ἀπροσίτῳ παρέχει.

with a strophe from Job:

> Shamáti khéllä rábbot:
> Menáchme 'amal koól' khem,
> Hakeç ledíberé rooch?
> Ma-yámriç'khá, ki táhnä?

The second characteristic of Hebrew poetry, which is occasionally to be found even in prose, is that repetition of the same thought in a slightly modified

---

[1] Ewald and others had conjectured long before that the colloquies of Job were in verse, but their attempts to reduce them to strophes were of a nature to weaken rather than confirm the theory. That the strophes consisted of four lines is a discovery of Prof. Bickell's. At first listened to with scepticism, it is now accepted by some of the leading critics of Germany, and received with favour by such English scholars as Prof. Cheyne.

form which is commonly known as parallelism. Thus, in the poem of Job the second line of the strophe expresses an idea very closely resembling that embodied in the first; and the third and fourth run parallel in like manner. For instance, Eliphaz, expounding the traditional teaching that the wicked man is punished in this life, says:

> "His offshoot shall wither before his time,
> And his branch shall not be green;
> He shall shake off his unripe grape, like the vine,
> And shall shed his flower, like the olive."

The second important aid to emendation is a careful comparison of the Hebrew text with the Greek translation known as the Septuagint (LXX.), which, undertaken and completed in Alexandria between the beginning of the third and the close of the second century B.C., offers the first recorded instance of an entire national literature being rendered into a foreign tongue. The extrinsic value of this work is obvious from the fact that it enables us to construct a text which is centuries older than that of which all our Hebrew manuscripts are servile copies, and is over a thousand years more ancient than the very oldest Hebrew codices now extant.[1] Not indeed that the poem of Job had undergone no changes between the time of its composition and the second century B.C.

---

[1] St. Paul in his quotations from the Old Testament usually follows the Septuagint. But the poem of Job he quotes from a lost version, some traces of which are to be found in the works of Clement of Alexandria.

On the contrary, some of the most important interpolations had already been inserted [1] and various excisions and transpositions made before the translator first took the work in hand. But at least the ground is cleared considerably, seeing that no less than four hundred verses which we now read in all our present Bibles, Hebrew and vernacular, were tacked on to the poem at a date subsequent to the Greek translation and therefore found no place in that version. These additions may, on the faith of the Septuagint, be struck out with all the less hesitation that both metre and parallelism confirm with their weighty testimony the trustworthy evidence of the orthodox translation that the strophes in question are insertions of a later date.

But the value of the Septuagint depends upon its greater or less immunity from those disfiguring changes which render the Hebrew text incomprehensible and from which few ancient works are wholly free. And unfortunately no such immunity can be claimed for it. What happened to the original text likewise befell the Greek translation. Desirous of putting an end to the disputes between Jews and Christians as to the respective merits of the two, a proselyte from Ephesus, Theodotion by name, undertook to do the Bible into

---

[1] "Inserted" is the strongest term that can be applied to editors who lived in a time when to foist one's own elucubrations upon a deceased genius was a work of piety deserving praise. Some of the acts which were virtues in Job's days have assumed a very different aspect in ours; but good intentions are always at a premium, and the Jewish interpolators were animated by the best.

Greek anew somewhere between 180-192 A.D. The basis of his work was the Septuagint, of which he changed nothing that in his opinion could stand; but at the same time he consulted the Hebrew manuscripts and vainly endeavoured to effect a compromise between the two. Among other innovations, he inserted in his translation the four hundred interpolated verses which, having been added to the Hebrew text after it had been first rendered into Greek, could not possibly have formed part of the Septuagint version. Later on (232–254 A.D.) Origen, anxious to throw light upon the cause of the divergences between existing translations and the original text, and to provide the means of judging of the respective merits of these, undertook one of those wearisome works of industry, which later on constituted a special feature of the activity of the Benedictine monks. The result of his researches was embodied in the Hexapla—a book containing, in six parallel columns, the original text in Hebrew and in Greek letters, the Greek translation by Aquila, another by Symmachus, the text of the Septuagint edited by himself, and Theodotion's version. Now Origen, acting upon the gratuitous assumption that the passages wanting in the Septuagint had formed part of the original Book of Job and had been omitted by the translators solely because they failed to understand their meaning, took them from Theodotion and incorporated them in his edition of the Septuagint as it appeared in the Hexapla, merely distinguishing them by means of asterisks. Unfortunately, in the course of time these distinctive marks disappeared partially or wholly, thus depriving the old Greek translation of its inestimable value as an aid to text criticism; and there remained but five manuscripts in which they were to some extent preserved.[1]

Until recently it was generally taken for granted by Biblical scholars that there were no codices extant in the world but these five, which contained data of a nature to enable us to reconstruct the text of the Septuagint. And the assistance given by these manuscripts was dubious at best, for they included the misleading additions incorporated in the text by Origen, merely marking them with asterisks, which were not only insufficient in number, but oftentimes wrongly distributed. No one ventured to hope that there was still extant a version from which the spurious verses were rigorously excluded. And the discovery of such a text by my friend, Prof. Bickell, marks a new epoch in the history of Biblical criticism.

One day that distinguished scholar, while sauntering about Monte Pincio with the late Coptic Bishop, Agapios Bsciai, was informed by this dignitary that he had found and transcribed a wretched codex of the Saidic [2] Version of Job in the Library of the Propaganda. Hearing that numerous passages were wanting in the newly discovered codex, Prof. Bickell at once conjectured that this "defective" version might possibly prove to be a translation of the original Septuagint text without the later additions; and having studied it

---

[1] Two Greek, two Latin, and one Syriac.
[2] Also called the Thebaic Version.

at the bishop's house saw his surmise changed to certainty; the text was indeed that of the original Septuagint without the disfiguring additions inserted by Origen. The late Prof. Lagarde of Göttingen then applied for, and received, permission to edit this precious find; but owing to the desire conceived later on by Pope Leo XIII. that an undertaking of such importance should be carried out by an ecclesiastic of the Roman Catholic Church, Lagarde's hopes were dashed at the eleventh hour, and Monsignor Ciasca, to whom the task was confided, accomplished all that can reasonably be expected from pious zeal and patient industry.

The Saidic version, therefore, as embodying a purer and more ancient text of the Book of Job than any we had heretofore possessed, is one of the most serviceable of the instruments employed in restoring the poem to its primitive form.[1] It frequently enables us to eliminate passages which formerly rendered the author's meaning absolutely incomprehensible, and at other times replaces obscure with intelligible readings which, while differing from those of the Massoretic manuscripts, are obviously the more ancient.

---

[1] As a translation it is a poor performance.

INTERPOLATIONS

HAVING thus briefly sketched the instruments by means of which the reconstruction of the poem of Job was undertaken, it may not be amiss to illustrate the manner in which they are employed in the light of a few examples. To begin with the structure of the metre. In the Authorised Version we find (chap. xii. 12) the words: "With the ancient is wisdom, and in length of days understanding." This in Hebrew is

>Bishíshim chókhma
>Veórekh yámim t'búna.

The first line therefore has five instead of seven syllables and is consequently defective; something must have fallen out. This conclusion, based upon the laws of the metre, is fully borne out by a study of the context; for it is enough to read Job's reply from the beginning to see that he could not have set himself to prove, as he is here made to do, that God is as wise as man; his contention really being that man's knowledge is ignorance compared with the wisdom of the Being who governs the universe. For he is arguing against the traditionalists who assert that justice is the essential characteristic of the conduct of the world, a thesis refuted by almost everything we see and hear around us. Bildad besought his sorely tried friend to learn of bygone generations and to view things through their eyes. "Shall they not teach thee?" he asks (viii. 10), to which Job's reply is an emphatic negative: "There is *no* wisdom with the ancient, nor understanding in length of days." To agree with his "friend" would be to throw up his case, and this the Authorised Version makes him do. God alone is endowed with wisdom; but is He likewise good? To this question His government of the universe alone can furnish an answer. There must evidently then have been a negative particle in the text which a copyist, shocked at the seemingly rash assertion, expunged. If now we add the words "for not" the metre is in order and the sense perfect:

> Ki én bishíshim chókhma
> V'córekh yámim t'búna.

Take another instance. The first part of v. 14, chap. xiv. is rendered in our version as follows: "If a man die shall he live again?" and the translation would be faithful enough if the Hebrew word were *hayichyä*, as our MSS. testify, but as an interrogation would destroy the parallelism of the strophe, it is evident that the syllable *ha*, which in Hebrew consists of one and not two letters, is an interpolation, and the word should be *yichyä* and the strophe (composed of v. 13 and 14a).

> "Oh, that thou wouldst hide me in the grave!
> That thou wouldst secrete me till thy wrath be passed!
> That thou wouldst appoint me a set time, and remember me!
> If so be man could die and yet live on."

Again starting from the recognised principle that the entire poem is composed on a regular plan and consists exclusively of four-line strophes, it is obvious that all the tristichs in chapters xxiv. and xxx. must be struck out. The circumstances that their contents are as irrelevant to the context as would be a number of stanzas of "The Ancient Mariner" if introduced into "Paradise Lost," that in form they are wholly different from the strophes of the poem of Job, and that there is obviously a sudden break in the text of the latter just when heterodoxy merges into blasphemy, have forced critics to the conclusion—about which there is hardly any difference of opinion—that these tristichs are extracts from a very different work, which were inserted to fill up the void created by orthodox theologians of a later date.[1]

Besides the four hundred verses which must be excluded on the ground that they are wanting in the Septuagint Version, and were therefore added to the text at a comparatively recent period,[2] the long-winded

[1] Chap. xxiv. 5-8, 10-24 and chap. xxx. 3-7 take the place of Job's blasphemous complaint about the unjust government of the world.

[2] For the benefit of readers who shrink from making any alteration in the Bible, and who are mostly unaware that innumerable and wide-reaching changes were effected in it by the negligence or design of scribes, theologians, and others, it may be well to point out that none of the changes rendered necessary by the reconstruction of the Books of Job and Ecclesiastes in any way affects whatever degree of inspiration they feel disposed to attribute to the Bible as a whole, or to the interpolations in particular. The point of view of the critic, if by no means identical with that of the pious worshipper, need not to clash with it. An interpolation may be—

discourse of Elihu [1] must be struck out, most of which was composed before the book was first translated into Greek. Common sense, unaided by any critical apparatus, suffices to mark this tedious monologue as an interpolation. The poet knew nothing of him who is supposed to have uttered it. In the prologue in prose where all the actors in this psychological drama are enumerated and described, Elihu is not once alluded to; and in the epilogue, where all the debaters are named and censured, he alone is absolutely ignored. Nay, it is evident that when Jahveh's discourse was written, the poet had no suspicion of the existence of this fourth friend; for at the conclusion of the "fourth friend's" pretentious speech, composed of scraps borrowed from those of the other actors in the drama, Jahveh addressed all present in a form of words which implies that not Elihu but Job was the last speaker, and had only that instant terminated his reply. This fact alone should be conclusive. But it is confirmed by other weighty considerations which leave no place for doubt. Thus, Elihu's style is *toto cœlo* different from that of the other parts of the poem: artificial, vague, rambling, prosaic, and strongly coloured by Aramaic idioms, while his doctrinal peculiarities, particularly his mention of interceding

---

and as we here see very often is — much more orthodox than an original text, and the more recent its origin the greater the chances that it will be so.

[1] xxxii.–xxxvii. In the Septuagint Version Elihu's discourse occupies but little more than half the number of verses to be found in the Hebrew manuscript and in the Authorised Version.

angels, while they coincide with those of the New Testament, are absolutely unknown to Job and his friends. Moreover, if Elihu had indeed formed one of the *dramatis personæ* of the original work, the *rôle* he would and should have assumed is not dubious; he must be the wise man according to the author's own heart. This he is or nothing. And yet, if he were really this, we should have the curious spectacle of the poet developing at great length an idea which runs directly counter to the fundamental conception underlying the entire work. For Elihu declares Job's sufferings to be a just punishment for his sins; whereas the poet and Jahveh Himself proclaim him to be the type of the just man, and describe his misery as a short, unmerited and exceptional probation. Evidently then Elihu is the elaborate production of some second-rate writer and first-class theologian awkwardly wedged into the poem perhaps a century or more after it had been composed, and certainly before the work was first translated into Greek.

The confusion introduced into the text by this insertion is bewildering in the extreme; and yet the result is but a typical specimen of the inextricable tangle which was produced by the systematic endeavours of later and pious editors to reduce the poem to the proper level of orthodoxy. Another instance is to be found in Job's reply to the third discourse of Bildad: in two passages of this discourse the hero completely and deliberately gives away the case which he had been theretofore so warmly defending, and accepts—to reject it later on as a matter of course—

the doctrine of retribution.[1] Now, on the one hand, if we remove these verses, Job's speech becomes perfectly coherent and logical, and the description of wisdom falls naturally into its right place; but, on the other hand, we have no reason whatever to call their authenticity in question and to strike them out. The solution of this difficulty is that Zophar who, in our versions, speaks but twice, really spoke three times, like each of his three colleagues, and that the verses in question were uttered by him, and not by Job. His discourse was intentionally split up into two portions, and incorporated in a speech delivered by Job, in order to represent the hero as an advocate of the dogma of retribution.

Another example of obviously intentional transposition occurs in chap. xl. where two verses are introduced as one of Job's replies to God, so as to allow of the latter delivering a second speech and utilising therein a fine description of the hippopotamus and the crocodile. Lastly, it needs little critical acumen to perceive that the scraps of dialogue attributed to Jahveh in the Hebrew text and Authorised Version are, in so far as they can claim to be regarded as authentic, but fragments of a single discourse. It would be preposterous to hold a poet or even an average poetaster responsible for the muddle made by the negligence of copyists and the zeal of interpolators who sought thus awkwardly to improve the author's theology at the cost of his poetry. But it is enough to consider the elements of this particular

---

[1] xxvii. 8-10, 14-23.

question for a moment to perceive that there can be but one solution. Jahveh makes a long and crushing reply to Job, gradually merges into fine descriptive but irrelevant poetry, and then suddenly calls for a rejoinder. The hero, humbled to the dust, exclaims[1] that he is vile and conscious of his impotence, and will lay his hand upon his mouth and open his lips no more. Here the matter should end, for Job has confessed himself vanquished. But no, Jahveh, instead of being touched by this meek avowal and self-humiliation, must needs address the human worm as if he had turned against his Creator, and asks such misplaced questions as "Hast thou an arm like God?" As a matter of fact, Jahveh, whose apparition is but a poetic symbol of the sudden flash of light which illumined the mind of the despairing hero, spoke but once. For Job, one glimpse through the veil was enough, one rapid glance at the realm where all is dark, and deep lies

"under deep unknown,
And height above unknown height."

---

[1] xl. 4–5.

JOB'S THEOLOGICAL AND PHILOSOPHICAL CONCEPTIONS

ALTHOUGH the main object of the poet is to present in a clear, comprehensive and palpable form the sphinx riddle of human existence, his work abounds nevertheless in a variety of interesting data, which throw considerable light upon the philosophical and theological theories in vogue among the thoughtful spirits of the Jewish community. Their " natural philosophy" offers little that is likely to interest and nothing of a nature to instruct the well-informed reader of to-day. But the mythological concreteness and palpitating vitality of all its elements profoundly impress us, less because of the curious standard they supply by which to gauge the intellectual level of that age than as the symbols chosen by the poet to express the identity and nothingness of all things living and inanimate. Before God, all creatures think, reason, speak, like man, because all are equal to him and he is but a breath. The stars, which are relatives of the Satan and of God's own children, wax enthusiastic and shout for joy; the lightning hearkens to the voice of its Creator and, flashing athwart the heavens, announces its presence. The sun is in continual danger of being devoured by a rapacious monster upon whom a watch has to be set; and all things live and move in the same way and by exactly the same force that dwells and acts in man with whom they are one in essence; and he himself is but a flower that sprouts, fades and dies.[1] Death is the end of man and beast and flower and grass alike; and after death comes dismal darkness. There is no difference among them. Man is no more and no less than all the rest. *Sheol*, or the realm of the dead, is a murky, silent and dreary abode, the shadowy inmates of which are as if they were not, unconscious as infants " which never saw the light."

This state, which is not perhaps absolutely equivalent to complete annihilation, is yet identical with that of "an hidden untimely birth." Translated into the language of philosophy this somewhat vague notion might be expressed as follows: All things, past, present and to come, which flit as unreal shadows on the wall of time and space, are manifestations of the one sole force which is everlasting and omnipresent. They are not parts of a whole which is one and divisible: all that we see and know of them in life is nothing; and after death they are what they were before—identical with the one.

> "One life through all the immense creation runs,
> One spirit is the moon's, the sea's, the sun's;
> All forms in the air that fly, on the earth that creep,
> And the unknown nameless creatures of the deep—
> Each breathing thing obeys one mind's control,
> And in all substance is a single soul."

---

[1] Strophe cxxi.

For Job's theory of the universe is dynamic and recognises but one force, which is so vague and indefinite that he hesitates to bestow upon it the name of the concrete God of the Jews.[1] There is no multiplicity, no duality, no other substance, no other cause. The One is and does alone. All things are shadowy delusions; He alone is real. We are nothing except in Him. Evil as well as good is His work. The Satan who tortures Job is one of the sons of God to whom special power is exceptionally delegated; but, as a rule, God Himself punishes the just and showers His blessings on the wicked. Everything that happens is the outcome of His will. There is no nature, no causation, no necessary law in the physical world; every event is the embodiment of the one will which is absolutely free, and therefore, neither to be foreseen nor explained.

Like Koheleth, Job seems to hold that intelligence is something secondary not primordial. Man, who is richly endowed with it on earth, knows really nothing, never can know anything, about the origin and reason of things. They are absolutely unknowable. He finds abyss yawning under abyss, height towering above height, and dark mysteries encompass him everlastingly.

> "But wisdom—whence shall it come?
> And where is the place of understanding?
> It is hid from the eyes of all living" (cxxxiv.).

And if there be at most but will-o'-the-wisps on this

---

[1] Lagarde seems to have hit the mark when he affirms that the poet's faith in God reduces itself to a vague belief in the divine.

side of the shadow of Night, there is nought but absolute darkness beyond.

These considerations would seem to offer a very satisfactory explanation of the monotheism of the poet which is far in advance of that of his contemporaries, to whatever age we may assign him. It is a purely philosophical conception which never was and never can be enshrined in a theological dogma, and to seek for its genesis in the evolution of the Jewish religion is far less reasonable than to derive it from the philosophy of the Greeks or the Hindoos.

Job's theory of ethics differs widely from that of his friends and contemporaries, and indeed from that of the bulk of mankind of all times. The Jews believed in fleeting pleasures and pains in this life as the sole recompense for virtue and sin; their modern heirs and successors hope for eternal bliss or fear everlasting suffering in the next. The motives deducible from both creeds are identical, and philosophy connotes them as egotism. Whether the meed I long for or the pain I would shun be transitory or everlasting, the moment my individual well-being becomes the motive of my conduct it is not easy to perceive where morality comes in. And so universally is egotism to be found at the root of what appear to us to be the most generous actions, that the Adversary was right enough in refusing, without conclusive proof, to enrol Job's name in the short list of exceptions. But Job's ethics were many degrees above proof. In no book of the ancient Testament and in no religion or philosophy of the old world, if we except Buddhism, do we find anything to compare with the sublime morality inculcated in the poem that bears his name. It utterly ignores the convenient and profitable virtue known as "duty to one's self" and bases all the other virtues on pity for our fellows, who are not merely our brethren but our very selves. The truly moral man should be able to say with Job:

> "I delivered the poor that cried aloud,
> And the orphan and him that had none to help him;
> And I gladdened the heart of the widow (ccxlvii.).
>
> I became eyes to the blind,
> And I was feet unto the lame (ccxlviii.).
>
> If I saw one perish for lack of clothing,
> Or any of the poor devoid of covering;
> Then surely did his loins bless me,
> And he was warmed with the fleece of my sheep (cclxix.).
>
> I have never made gold my hope (cclxxi.).
>
> Never did I rejoice at the ruin of my hater,
> Nor exult when misery found him out (cclxxiii.).
>
> Did not he that made me in the womb, make him? (cclxvii.).
>
> Did I not weep for him that was in trouble?" (cclix.).

And having accomplished all this without fear of pain,

> "Gaze onward without claim to hope,
> Nor, gazing backward, court regret."

This is the only system of morality deserving that much-abused name; it was preached and to a great extent practised in India by the Jainists and the Buddhists, and for the first time in the Old Testament by the author of our poem.

All the ills and sorrows of life, merited and

unmerited alike, Job is prepared for. They are the commonplaces of human existence and as inseparable from it as shadow from light. But what he cannot endure is the thought that his good name, the sole comfort left him in his misery, shall be sacrificed to a theological theory which runs counter to every fact of public history and private experience. This is an injustice which seems to strike at the root of all morality, and he passionately attacks all who uphold it, even though God Himself be of the number. For he has unshaken faith in eternal justice as something independent even of the deity. Its manifestations may be imperceptible and incomprehensible to us, but it governs the universe all the same, and faith in this fact was his lodestar when sun and moon had gone out and the aimless tornado raged around and ghastly horrors issued from the womb of Night. The wicked may prosper and the just man die on a dunghill, scorned by all and seemingly forsaken by God Himself, but it is none the less true that sin and suffering, virtue and reward are fruits of the same tree, one and indivisible. They are the manna the taste of which adapts itself to the eater. Job expresses the conviction, which St. Bernard so aptly formulated when he said: "Nought can harm me but myself;" and it is this conviction that nerves and sustains him in his defiant challenge to the Most High and prompts his appeal to eternal justice against even God Himself:

> "Will he plead against me with his almighty power?
> If not, then not even he would prevail against me.
> For a righteous one would dispute with him." (ccxvi.)

But after the theophany, when the truth has dawned upon the mind of the heroic sufferer, he sees that eternal justice needs not even this certificate of its existence, that it can dispense with the most eloquent human advocate, and he waives what he had theretofore held to be his indefeasible right and puts the crown on his system of ethics by enduring his lot in silence.

Peace grounded on knowledge, therefore, is the end of Job's doubts and misgivings. But it is not the knowledge of a reward to come, a presentiment of the joys of heaven, of an everlasting feeding-trough where our hunger and thirst for existence shall be satiated for ever and ever. It is that sobering knowledge which is increase of sorrow. Injustice in the world there is none; if all beings living are liable to pain, and everything animate and inanimate is subject to decay and death, the reason is that suffering and dissolution are the conditions of existence, which is therefore an evil. To desire the one is to wish for or accept the other. This is the conviction which brings peace to the soul of the hero and enables him to exclaim:

> "I resign and console myself,
> Though in dust and ashes."

ANALYSIS OF THE POEM

THE popular legend of Job, which was current among the Hebrews and probably among their Semitic neighbours for centuries before the poem was composed, is embodied in the prologue and epilogue,[1] which are written in prose. The data it contains are utilised by the author for the purpose of clearly stating, not of elucidating, the main problem, and it would be a grave mistake on the part of the reader to attempt to supplement the reasoning of Job's friends by arguments drawn from the details narrated in the legend. Thus, the conversation between Jahveh and the Satan is obviously intended to establish the all-important fact that Job, although not a member of the chosen people, a believer in their priestly dogmas, nor an observer of their religious rites and ceremonies, was none the less a truly just man, the perfect type of the righteous of all times and countries. On the other hand, the circumstances that his sufferings were no more than a probation, and that they were followed by fabulous wealth and intensified happiness, are dismissed by the

---

[1] The prologue is contained in chaps. i.-ii.; the epilogue in chap. xlii. 7-17 of our English Bibles.

poet as wholly irrelevant to the question at issue. Nor, considering their purely exceptional character, would they have tended in any degree to solve it. If Job's misery was an ordeal, all unmerited suffering cannot be pressed into the same convenient category. His individual privations and pains may have been compensated for by subsequent plenty and prosperity; but there are other just men who rot on the dunghill and die in despair. The author, therefore, wisely refrained from drawing on the legend more extensively than was absolutely needful for the materials of his poem, and from thus reducing a universal problem to the dimensions of an individual case.

The folk-story of the just man, Job, is conceived in the true spirit of Eastern legendary lore. The colours are laid on with an ungrudging hand. He was not merely well-to-do and contented, he was the happiest mortal who had ever walked the earth in his halcyon days, and the most hopelessly wretched during his probation.

But although wont, as the Preacher recommends, to fill up his cup with the wine of life, "pressing all that it yields of mere vintage," he was anything but an egotist. The broad stream of his sympathy flowed out towards all his fellows, nay, to all things animate and inanimate. The sheep, the lion, the eagle, and the oxen, were his comrades, the fire and the wind his kinsmen. Even for his worst enemies he had no curse, nor did he ever rejoice in their merited misfortunes. So blameless and upright was his living and working, so completely had he eschewed even heart-sins, that he might have carried windows in his breast that all might see what was being done within.

Now, in accordance with the retribution-theory then in fashion—small temporary profits and quick returns—he had amply merited his good fortune, and might have reasonably expected to enjoy it to the close of a long life, which for him was the end of everything. In fact, he had no longer any serious grounds for apprehending the gathering of clouds of misfortune to darken the sunshine of his existence, seeing that he had already attained to a ripe age, was possessed of vast herds of cattle and thousands of camels, was blest with a numerous family, and passed for "the greatest of all the children of the East." But the most specious theological theories are as powerless to guarantee the just man from the blows of adversity as to hinder the worm from finding the blushing rose's "bed of crimson joy"; and whether pain and sorrow be labelled "probation" or "just punishment," they will never cease to figure among the commonplaces of human existence.

At one of the social gatherings of the courtiers of heaven, Jahveh takes occasion to laud the virtue of the just man, Job, whereupon the Satan, who not only understands, but sees through the righteousness of the bulk of mankind, expresses his conviction that it has its roots in mere selfishness. Jahveh then empowers the Adversary to put it to the test by depriving Job of his possessions and his family. On this, the hero's wealth and happiness vanished as suddenly as the smile on the face of an infant, and in a twinkling, so to say, he was changed into a perfect type of human wretchedness.

By one of those extraordinary miracles which are characteristic of Oriental fiction, in the course of a single day Job's four hundred yoke of oxen were seized and carried off by the Sabeans, his seven thousand scattered sheep were sought out and consumed by lightning, his three thousand camels were driven away by Chaldeans, and his sons and daughters killed by the falling of a house. Being but human, Job's soul is harrowed up by grief; but, recognising the emptiness of all things, he endures his lot manfully and without murmur or complaint.

When the sons of God met again in the council chamber of heaven, Jahveh triumphantly inquired of the Adversary what he now thought of Job's virtue and its taproot. But the Satan still clung tenaciously to his low view of the mainspring of the hero's conduct. "Skin for skin, yea, all that a man hath will he give for his life. But put forth thine hand now, and touch his bone and his flesh, and he will renounce thee to thy face. And the Lord said unto the Adversary: Behold he is in thine hand; only spare his life." Whereupon he was smitten with the most loathsome disease known in the East, which together with the moral suffering resulting from utter abandonment, besieged him, "even to the gates and inlets of his life." But firm and manful, with strength nurtured by the witness of his own conscience, and the conviction that true virtue is independent of reward, he maintains the citadel unconquered, refusing to open the portals even to Jahveh Himself.

Nothing can subdue Job, not even the bitter fruits of the diabolical refinement of the Adversary who, having permission to slay all the hero's kith and kin, spares his spouse, lest misery should harbour any possibilities unrealised.

At last three of Job's friends come from the uttermost ends of the earth to visit and console him. Travelling over enormous distances, and setting out from opposite points of the compass, they all contrive to reach the sufferer at the same moment; and at the sight of the deformed and loathsome figure of their friend are all three struck dumb with grief. Without any previous consultation among themselves, they sit silent and sad for seven days and seven nights, gazing with fascinated horror on the misshapen figure on the dunghill. This curious manifestation of friendship unmans the hero whose fortitude had been proof against the most cruel physical and moral suffering; utterly breaking down, he "fills with woes the passing wind," and bitterly curses his existence. Awe at first keeps him from censuring God's ways; truthfulness from condemning himself. He cannot understand why he suffers, whether there be any truth or none in the traditional doctrine of unfailing retribution upon earth; for he has certainly done everything to merit happiness and nought to deserve punishment. Society, however, is there in the person of his friends to dispel this delusion. They hold a brief for the cut-and-dried theology of the day which tells them that in Job there was a reservoir of guilt and sin filling up from youth to age, which now, no longer able to hold its loathsome charge, burst and overwhelmed with misery their friend and his family. They play their parts very skilfully, at first softly stroking, as it were, the beloved friend, as if to soothe his pain, and then vigorously rubbing the salt in the gaping wounds of the groaning victim.

The campaign is opened mildly by Eliphaz, a firm believer in the spooks and spectres of borderland, who, in reply to Job's complaint, assures his friend that no really innocent human being ever died in misery as he now seems to be dying, and gently reminds him that "affliction shooteth not from the dust, neither doth trouble sprout up from the ground;" they need the fertile soil of sin, which Job must have provided, unknown to his easy-going friends who, taking him at his own estimation, heretofore considered him a just man. But even if he were what he would have them believe he is, he has no ground for just complaint: for "happy is the man whom God correcteth." To this the hero replies, accentuating his innocence, and pouring forth his plaint in "wild words," for God "useth me as an enemy." He seeks not for mercy, he explains, but for justice, nay, he is magnanimous enough to be content with even less. He only asks of God,

"That it would please him to destroy me,
That he would let go his hand and cut me off;"[1]

and this request having been refused, suicide, the ever "open door" of the Stoics, invited him temptingly in,

---

[1] Strophe xxxv.

but he withstood the temptation, and comforted himself with the knowledge that all things in time have an end.

> "My soul would have chosen strangling,
> And death by my own resolve.
> But I spurned it; for I shall not live for ever."[1]

The arbitrary and incomprehensible will of the deity may, in ultimate analysis, be the changeful basis of right and wrong, but, if so, divine justice differs from human not merely in degree but likewise in character, and not apparently to its advantage. The tuneful Psalmist had sung in ecstatic wonder at the mercy of God: "What is man, that thou art mindful of him? and the son of man that thou visitest him? For thou hast made him a little lower than the angels, and hast crowned him with glory and honour."[2] Job, having looked upwards in the same direction, not for mercy but for simple justice, and looked in vain, parodies with bitter irony those same verses of the Psalm:

> "What is man that thou shouldst magnify him?
> And that thou shouldst set thine heart upon him?
> That thou shouldst visit him every morning,
> And try him every moment?"[3]

Bildad, the Traditionalist *par excellence*, then addresses a sharp reproof to the just man who refused to recognise as mercy in God the conduct which, were a man responsible for it, he must needs condemn as wickedness. He bids him inquire of bygone generations

---

[1] Strophe lii. [2] Psa. viii. 4, 5. [3] Strophe liii.

what they thought of the goodness of the Creator, and asks him to be guided by the wisdom of his forefathers, who lived and throve on the spiritual food of retribution which he now rejects with loathing. This attack provokes a new outburst on the part of Job, who ironically paraphrases and develops the ideas of his comforters, deriding the notion that the deity can change right into wrong or that true morality needs the divine will as a basis.

> "How should man be in the right against God?
> If he long to contend with him,
> He cannot answer him one of a thousand."[1]

> "Lo, he glideth by me and I see him not;
> And he passeth on, but I perceive him not."[2]

His friends had recommended him to pray for pardon and repent, and had promised him the return of his happiness as a consequence. But Job scouts the idea. His righteousness, if he indeed possess it, is his own; no prayers can add to, no punishment can take from, that.

> "I must make supplication unto his judgment,
> Who doth not answer me, though I am righteous!"[3]

And as for a God who being almighty is yet unjust, prayer would be superfluous, no supplications would avail aught with Him; He would cause even incarnate holiness to appear wicked in its own eyes.

> "Though I were just, my own mouth would condemn me;
> Though I were faultless, he would make me crooked."

---

[1] Strophe lxv.   [2] Strophe lxix.   [3] Strophe lxxi.

For even the will of a created being is in the hands of its Creator, and is not, cannot be, free. Job feels and knows that he is right-minded and good, and he puts the testimony of his own conscience above the decrees of any beings, human or divine, which, whatever else they may achieve, cannot shake the foundations of true justice and morality, which are eternal.

> "Faultless I am, I set life at naught;
> I spurn my being, therefore I speak out."[1]

And the outcome of his outspokenness is a solemn charge of injustice against God,[2] a sigh of profound regret that he was ever born into this miserable world, and a wish that his sufferings might "come to an end before he should return to the land of darkness and of gloom" whence he came.

After this, Zophar, the third comforter, opens his lips for coarse vituperation rather than sharp rebuke, and regrets that God Himself does not feel moved to give a practical lesson of wisdom to the conceited "prattler," who persists in believing in his own innocence in spite of the unmistakable judgment of his just Creator and the unanimous testimony of his candid friends. Job's reply to this vigorous advocate of God is even more powerful and indignant than any of the foregoing. He repeats and emphasises his indictment against the Deity. No omnipotent being who was really just and good could approve, or even connive at, much less practise, the scandalous injustice which

---

[1] Strophe lxxiii.   [2] Strophes lxxiv-lxxviii.

characterises the conduct of the universe and the so-called moral order, and of which his own particular grievances are a specimen. Not that the curious spectacle that daily meets our eye, wherein wickedness and hypocrisy are prosperous and triumphant while truth and integrity are trampled under foot, is necessarily incompatible with absolute and eternal justice; it is irreconcileable only with the attributes of a personal deity, an almighty and just creator, who would necessarily be responsible for these evils as for all things else, if he existed. If the world be the work of an omnipotent maker, its essential moral characteristic partakes of the nature of his attributes; and the main moral feature of our world is evil, and not good. This is the ever-recurring refrain of Job's discourses. Nor does he hesitate when occasion offers to proclaim his conviction in the plainest of plain language, for he entertains no fear of what may further befall him.

> "Lo, let him kill me, I cherish hope no more,
> Only I will justify my way before his face."[1]

The three friends return a second time to the charge, each one speaking in the same order as before, and each one eliciting a separate reply, in which Job reaffirms his innocence, reiterates his indictment against

---

[1] Strophe cxv. *Cf.* strophe clxix., where he dares his friend to prove him guilty of blasphemy when he is merely giving expression to the truth:

> " If indeed ye will glorify yourselves above me,
> And prove me guilty of blasphemy;
> Know, then, that God hath wronged me!"

the Most High, and reproaches his comforters with their off-hand condemnation of an attitude resulting from sufferings which they are slow to realise and from knowledge which they are unable to grasp. In his rejoinder to Zophar, he lays special stress upon the prosperity and success of the wicked who scoff at the laws of God and yet "while away their days in bliss." If God will not punish them, is He just? If He cannot, is He almighty? As He does not, why speak of the moral order of His world or of the moral attributes of Himself?

Eliphaz opens the third series of speeches by accusing his friend of selfishness, dishonesty, hard-heartedness and avarice, on no better grounds than the assumption that God's justice warrants us in believing that where punishment is inflicted there also must sin have been committed. Job, instead of condescending to refute the charge, ironically admits it, and then bitterly remarks that he would like to know how God would justify His conduct and convict him of sin if only they both could argue out the question together on terms of equality. But in all the universe he looks for God in vain:

"Behold, I go forward, but he is not there,
And backward, but I cannot perceive him."[1]

Bildad then proceeds to emphasise the omnipotence of the Creator with whom the human worm, the maggot, dares to enter into judgment, and Job replies to all three, refuting them out of their own mouths. His

---

[1] Strophe ccxvii.

conscience, he tells them, is proof sufficient of his right conduct, whereas his misery, by their own admission, proves nothing at all.

> "Till I die, I will not yield up my integrity!
> My righteousness I hold fast, and will not let it go,
> My heart doth not censure any one of my days."[1]

As for the argument from punishment to sin, all three friends had in the course of their speeches laid it down that the lines on which the universe is governed are known to no man. If this be so, who are they that have surprised the secret and found the clue to the enigma? Who revealed to them that retribution is the basis of the moral order? Man knows nothing, can never hope to know anything, of the inner working of the world, of the why and the wherefore of our miserable being and of the existence of all things. The Godhead alone could fathom these mysteries,[2] if He existed.

Job takes no notice of the succeeding brief remarks of Zophar in his final and longest discourse which, replete with sorrowful reminiscences of his past happy life, is less defiant than any of those that preceded. Wandering in thought through the necropolis of buried hopes, fears and achievements, he seems to inhale an atmosphere of soothing melancholy that softens and subdues his wild passion. The vibration

---

[1] Strophe ccxxx.

[2] As Professor Bickell rightly remarks: "At bottom what Job means is, that God alone knows the meaning of our sorrowful existence, if, indeed, He does know it" ("Das Buch Job," p. 5).

of past efforts and of deeds long since done, trembling along his tortured frame, causes even saddest thoughts to blend with sweet sensations. Then turning from what once was to what now is, and missing the logical nexus between the two states, he solemnly calls upon God to produce it, if He can:

> "Here is my signature; let the Almighty answer me,
> And hear the indictment which my adversary hath written."[1]

Scarcely has Job finished speaking when Jahveh appears in a whirlwind and the heart of the clouds is cloven by a voice of thunder startling the silent air. The purpose of His coming is to prove men's ignorance, not to enlighten it, at least not beyond the degree involved by affixing the highest seal to the negative views expressed by the hero. He plies Job with a number of questions on cosmology, astronomy, meteorology, &c., with a view to show that we are ignorant of the ultimate reason of even the most familiar objects and phenomena, and practically know nothing about anything. The natural conclusion is that they are unknowable, and that intellect, knowledge, consciousness, is something secondary, accidental, and as transitory as the life it accompanies. To make an exception in favour of Jahveh Himself, would be to lose sight of the important fact that His apparition was never meant by the poet to be taken literally.[2] It is

---

[1] Strophe cclxxvi.

[2] The mere circumstance that the Deity is no longer called by His usual name when He appears in the whirlwind is of itself an indication that the poet was not alluding to God.

neither more nor less than a symbol of the insight which Job obtains into the nature of things, of the light which enables him to see that there is naught but darkness now and for ever. He perceives by the simplest, clearest, and most conclusive of all mental processes, a direct intuition, the truth of the ideas to some of which he had but coldly assented before—viz., that things are but shadows and existence an evil; that underlying every being, animate and inanimate, there is a force existing outside the realm of time and space, and that it is at bottom identical with the human will; that eternal justice lies at the root of everything, is the ultimate basis of all existence; that the sufferings of men, innocent or guilty, and the prevalence of evil are incompatible with a personal creator; that intellect is secondary, and barely sufficient for the practical needs of life, after which it ceases to be an attribute of whatever of man may outlive his body; and, finally, that as we can know nothing beyond the bare fact that there is an absolute law of compensation from which there is no exemption, it behoves us to cultivate ethics rather than science, and to resign ourselves uncomplainingly to the inevitable.

However unpalatable these final conclusions may appear to pious readers accustomed to seek in the Book of Job for the most striking proofs of some of the principal teachings of the Christian dispensation, it is difficult, not to say impossible, to study the work in its restored form and arrive at any other. With Job, God and wisdom are synonymous. And of the latter he says:

> "But wisdom—whence shall it come?
> And where is the place of understanding?
> It is hid from the eyes of all living,
> Our ears alone have heard thereof."[1]

These words were uttered before he had obtained the insight which brought resignation in its train. He alludes to them in his last brief discourse.

> "I had heard of thee by the hearing of the ear,
> But now mine eye hath beheld thee;
> Therefore I resign and console myself,
> Though in dust and ashes."[2]

Professor Bickell puts the matter very lucidly in his short but comprehensive introduction to the poem: "As long as Job, solicitous for his understanding, demanded an explanation of his unutterable suffering, whereby the mysterious, piteous condition of mankind is shadowed forth, his seeking was vain, and he ran the risk of loosing himself in the problems of eternal justice, the worth of upright living, and even the existence of God; for an unjust, ruthless, almighty being is no God. But by means of the theophany—which is to be understood merely as a process in his own heart, and which clearly shows him the impotence of feeble man to unravel the world-enigmas—he attains to insight; not, indeed, of a positive kind such as a knowledge of the ways of God would confer, but negative insight by means of that resignation which flows from excess of pain. It is thus that his own heroic saying is fulfilled

---

[1] Strophe ccxxxiv.   [2] Strophe cccix.

about the reaction of unmerited suffering upon the just man."[1]

"But the righteous holds on his way,
And the clean-handed waxeth ever stronger."[2]

---

[1] *Cf.* Bickell, *op. cit.* pp. 8–9.   [2] Strophe clvi.

KOHELETH

'Αρχὴν μὲν μὴ φῦναι ἐπιχθονίοισιν ἄριστον
Μήδ' εἰσιδεῖν αὐγὰς ὀξέος ἠελίου.
Φύντα δ'ὅπως ὤκιστα πύλας 'Αΐδαο περῆσαι,
Καὶ κεῖσϑαι πολλὴν γῆν ἐπαμησάμενον.

THEOGNIS.

CONDITION OF THE TEXT

OF all the books of the Old Testament, not excepting the Song of Songs, none offers such rich materials to the historian of philosophy or such knotty problems to the philological critic as Koheleth[1] or Ecclesiastes. This interesting treatise is, in its commonly received shape, little more than a tissue of loose disjointed aphorisms and contradictory theses concerning the highest problems of ethics and metaphysics. The form of the work is characterised by an utter lack of plan; the matter by almost impenetrable obscurity. So completely entangled are the various threads of thought, that few commentators or critics possessed the needful degree of hope and courage to set about unravelling them. One paragraph, for instance, is saturated with Buddhistic pessimism; another breathes a spirit of religious resignation, of almost hearty hopefulness; this sentence lays down a universal principle which is absolutely denied by the next; the thesis is followed by proofs, in the very midst of which lurks the antithesis; a series of profound remarks upon one

---

[1] The most satisfactory translation of the word Koheleth is, the Speaker. "Preacher" conveys a modern and incorrect notion.

subject is suddenly interrupted by bald statements about another, the irrelevancy of which is suggestive of the ravings of a delirious fever patient. Thus one verse begins[1] by recommending men to make the most of their youth by following the bent of their inclinations and the desire of their eyes, such enjoyment being a gift of God,[2] and finishes by threatening all who act upon the advice with condign punishment to be ultimately dealt out by God Himself; and the very next verse proceeds to draw the logical conclusion, which oddly enough, runs thus: "*therefore* drive sorrow from thy heart, and put away evil from thy flesh." In one place[3] the writer solemnly and sadly affirms that the destiny of the upright and the wicked, the wise and the foolish is wholly alike; in another[4] he seems to proclaim that the unrighteous shall suffer for their evil-doing, while the God-fearing shall be rewarded with long life, which again he stoutly denies shortly before and immediately afterwards. It is impossible to read chap. ii. 11 and 12 without coming to the conclusion that we either have to do with the incoherent ravings of a disordered mind, or else that the leaves of the original manuscript were dislocated and then put together haphazard.[5] The "for" that connects the

---

[1] xi. 9.   [2] ii. 24.   [3] ix. 2.   [4] viii. 12, 13.

[5] The verses in question are: "11. Then I looked on all the works that my hands had wrought, and on the labour that I had laboured to do: and, behold, all *was* vanity and vexation of spirit, and *there was* no profit under the sun. 12. And I turned myself to behold wisdom, and madness, and folly: for what *can* the man *do* that cometh after the king *even* that which hath been already done."

seventh and eighth verses of chapter vi. is forcibly suggestive of the line of argument which made Tenterden Steeple the cause of Goodwin Sands, while the nexus between the sixth and seventh verses of chapter xi. is scarcely more obvious than that which is to be found between any two of the nonsense verses that amuse intelligent children in "Alice in Wonderland." And yet this production, in its present chaotic condition, has been, and is still, gravely attributed to the pen of King Solomon in his character as the ideal sage of humanity![1]

---

[1] Only, however, by the strictest of orthodox theologians, who admiringly attribute to the Holy Spirit a hopeless confusion of ideas which they would resent as insulting if predicated of themselves. As a matter of historic fact, Solomon, so far from meriting his reputation as a philosopher, was a rough-and-ready kinglet, who ruled his subjects with a rod of iron and ground them down with intolerable burdens.

PRIMITIVE FORM OF THE BOOK

THE desperate efforts of professional theologians to smooth away, explain, and reconcile all these incoherences and contradictions, constitute one of the most marvellous exhibitions of mental acrobatics recorded even in the history of hermeneutics. Many of these exegetes set out on the assumption that a revelation vouchsafed to Solomon could not possibly embody any statement incompatible with the truths of Christianity which emanate from the same eternal source; and they all firmly held that at the very least it must be in harmony with the fundamental dogmas common to Judaism and the teachings of Christ. In reality, what this generous hypothesis came to, whenever there was no question of text criticism involved, was a substitution of the human ideal for the divine execution. The best accredited contemporary theologians however, Catholic and non-Catholic, have insight enough to descry the stamp of true inspiration in a book which enshrines some of the highest truths laid down in the Sermon on the Mount combined with a good deal that obviously clashes with theological dogmas formulated at a much later date for the behoof of a very different social organism. In any case the original work, as it appears to have issued from the hand of "Koheleth," was composed in a spirit as conducive to true morality as the sublime eloquence of Isaiah or the absolute resignation of the author of the 73rd Psalm. Critics who succeeded in satisfactorily solving many of the philological, philosophical, and historical problems suggested by Koheleth utterly failed to find therein any traces of an intelligible plan. It was reserved to Professor Bickell, of Vienna, to point out what seem to be the true lines on which alone it is possible to arrive at a solution alike satisfactory to the reader and respectful to the author. His theory[1]—it is, and it can be no more than a theory—which has already received the adhesion of some of the most authoritative Bible scholars on the Continent, may be briefly summed up as follows : The present disordered condition of the book, Koheleth, is the result of the shifting of the sheets of the Hebrew manuscript from their original places and of the addition of a number of deliberate interpolations. The latter are of two kinds: those which seemed necessary for the purpose of supplying the cement required to join together the unconnected verses which, in consequence of the dislocation, were unexpectedly placed side by side, and the passages composed with the object of toning down, or serving as a counterpoise to the very unorthodox views of the writer.

---

[1] Professor Cheyne discusses Bickell's theory with the caution characteristic of English theology and the fairness of unprejudiced scholarship (" Job and Solomon," p. 273 fol.).

Professor Bickell's assumption involves no inherent improbability, runs counter to no ascertained facts, and is therefore perfectly tenable. What it supposes to have occurred to Koheleth has, in fact, often happened to other works, religious and profane. It can be conclusively shown, for instance, that certain leaves of the Book of Ecclesiasticus dropped, in like manner, from the Greek Codex, whereby three chapters were transposed from their original places; for the Latin and Syriac versions, which were made before the accident, still exhibit the original and only intelligible arrangement. An old Syriac manuscript of the poems of Isaac of Antioch, now in the Vatican Library, suffered considerably from a similar mishap, and various other cases in point have come under the notice of orientalists and archæologists.[1] In the present instance, what is believed to have taken place is this. The Hebrew Codex, of which no translation had as yet been made, consisted of a series of fascicules, each one of which contained four sheets once folded, or four double leaves, the average number of characters on each single leaf amounting to about 525.[2] The Codex, which most probably included other treatises preceding and following Koheleth, possessed an unknown number of fascicules, Koheleth beginning on the sixth leaf of one and ending on the third of the

---

[1] *Cf.* for instance, Cornill, "Theologisches Literaturblatt," Sept. 19, 1884.

[2] This mean estimate tallies with calculations made by the late Professor Lagarde for another book of the Old Testament.

fourth following. According to the hypothesis we are considering, the middle fascicules becoming loose, fell out of the Codex, and were found by some one who was utterly unqualified to replace them in position. This person took the inner half of the second,[1] folded it inside out, and then laid it in the new order[2] immediately after the first fascicule. Next came the inner sheet of the third fascicule,[3] followed by the outside half of the second,[4] in the middle of which the two double leaves, 13, 18, and 14, 17, had already been inserted.[5] Although the fourth fascicule had kept its place, it was not on this account preserved from the effects of the confusing changes caused by the loosening of the ligature, for between its two first leaves the remaining sheet of the third fascicule[6] found a place. Finally, leaf 17 becoming separated from its new environment, found a definite resting-place between 19 and 21.[7] The result of this dislocation was the utter disappearance of all trace of plan in the work, the incoherences of which would be still more numerous and glaring, had it not been for the transitional words and phrases that were soon after interpolated for the purpose of welding together passages that were never intended to dovetail.[8]

---

[1] The leaves 6, 7, 8, 9.   [2] The pages following each other thus: 8, 9, 6, 7.   [3] Leaves 15 and 16.   [4] 4, 5, 10, 11.   [5] So that the order was then: 4, 5, 13, 14, 17, 18, 10, 11.   [6] 12, 19.
[7] The sequence of the leaves was then; 1, 2, 3, 8, 9, 6, 7, 15, 16, 4, 5, 13, 14, 18, 10, 11, 20, 12, 19, 17, 21, 22.
[8] The most practical and simple way of realising Professor Bickell's theory is to make a little book of four fascicules of four

Such is the ingenious theory. The degree of probability attaching to it depends partly on the weight of corroborative evidence to be found in the book itself, and partly on the completeness with which it explains the many difficulties which the traditionalist view could but formulate. Thoroughly to sift and weigh this evidence, much of which is of a purely philological character, would require a book to itself; but it will not be amiss to give one or two instances of the nature of the arguments relied upon.

Chap. x. 1, in the present text, is wholly corrupt, owing to the circumstance that several interpolations were inserted in it at a later date. Now a little reflection suffices to show that these additions consist of words taken from chap. vii. 1. But if the book had been composed as it now stands, such a transposition would be practically impossible, because chap. x. is separated from chap. vii. by too great an interval. In the original sequence, however, which Prof. Bickell's theory

---

double leaves each. On these leaves write the contents of the original manuscript leaves in chapter and verse numbers. On each of the three last leaves of the first fascicule (counting, as in Hebrew, from right to left) write i. 1–ii. 11. On the first two leaves of the second fascicule write v. 9–vi. 7 (this must be written on each of the leaves, as it is not quite certain how they were divided). On third and fourth leaves of the second fascicule write iii. 9–iv. 8; on each of the fifth and sixth leaves, ii. 12–iii. 8. On the seventh and eighth leaves, viii. 6–ix. 3. Then comes the third fascicule. On the first leaf, write ix. 11–x. 1; on the second and third leaves, vi. 8–vii. 22 on the fourth and fifth leaves, iv. 9–v. 8; on the sixth leaf, x. 16–xi. 6; on the seventh leaf, vii. 23–viii. 5; on the eighth leaf, x. 2–15. Lastly comes the fourth fascicule. On the first leaf, ix. 3–10, on the second and third leaves, xi. 7–xii. 8.

supposes and restores, there was no difficulty. There the leaf ix. 11–x. 1 was followed by two leaves containing vi. 8–vii. 22, so that the words "precious," and "wisdom is better than glory," might have been easily shifted to x. 1 from the margin of vii. 1.

Again, in the primitive sequence viii. 4 was immediately followed by x. 2. After the dislocation of the leaves it was erroneously placed before viii. 6, a few words having been previously interpolated between the two, solely in the interests of orthodoxy.[1] In order to bridge over the gap between them, a transitional half verse was strung together, in an absolutely mechanical manner, from words that precede or follow. And the words that precede and follow are those which we find in the primitive arrangement of the manuscript, not in the present sequence. Thus, at the bottom of the leaf containing viii. 4, the first words, "leb chakham,"[2] of the following verse (x. 2) were inserted, and then by inadvertence repeated on the next leaf. Seeing these words, the author of the transition made them the subject of his new verse. He selected the grammatical objects of the sentence from the verse which follows in the new sequence,[3] and took the verb from the preceding half verse, which is itself an older interpolation.

Lastly, Koheleth's treatise, which in our Bibles is utterly devoid of order or sequence, falls naturally, in

---

[1] The first half of viii. 5: "Whoso keepeth the commandment shall feel no evil thing." This interpolation is older than the accident to the MS.   [2] The heart of the wise.   [3] viii. 6.

its restored form, into two distinct halves: a speculative and a practical, distinguished from each other by characteristics proper to each, which there is no mistaking. The former, for instance, contains but few metrical passages, whereas the latter is composed of poetry and prose in almost equal proportions. The ethical part continually addresses the reader himself in the second person singular, while the discursive section never does. In a word, internal evidence leaves no doubt that, whether the dislocation of the chapters was the result of accident or design, this was the ground plan of the original treatise.

KOHELETH'S THEORY OF LIFE

READ in its primitive shape, the book is a systematic disquisition on the questions, What positive boon has life in store for us? to which the emphatic answer is "None;" and How had we best occupy the vain days of our wretched existence? which the author solves by recommending moderate sensuous enjoyment combined with healthy activity. He begins his gloomy meditations with a general survey of the wearisome working of the machinery of the world, wherein is neither rest nor profit. Everything is vanity, and the pursuit of wind.[1] Existence in all its myriad forms is an aimless, endless, hopeless endeavour. The very clod of earth manifests its striving, in gravitation, for the attainment of a central point without dimensions, which, if realised, would entail its own annihilation; the solids tend to become liquids, the liquids to resolve themselves in vapour. The plant grows from germ through stem and leaf to blossom and fruit, which last is but the beginning of a new germ that again develops through flower to fruit, and so on for ever and ever. In animals, life is the same restless, aimless, unsatisfied striving, in the first place

---

[1] i. 2-11.

after reproduction, followed by the death of the individual and the appearance of a new one which in turn runs through all the stadia of the old. The very matter of all organisms is ever changing. As for man, his whole life is but one long series of yearnings after objects, each one of which presents itself to his will as the one great goal until attained, whereupon it is cast aside to make way for another. We know what we long for to-day, we shall know what we shall seek to-morrow; but what the human race supremely desires, its ultimate aim and end, no man can say. Existence is a futile beating of the air, a clutching of the wind. The living make way for the unborn, the dead nourish the living; no one possesses ought that was not torn from some other being; strife and hate, evil and pain are the commonplaces of existence; life and death follow each other everlastingly. All striving is want and therefore suffering, until it is satisfied, when it assumes the form of disappointment; for no satisfaction is lasting. In a word, the universe is a wheel that revolves on its axis for ever—and there is no ultimate aim or end in it all.[1] Knowledge, wisdom, and enjoyment, each of which Koheleth characterises by a distich, are likewise vain, or worse. What, then, is the secret of "happiness"? Surely not wealth, which the Preacher himself having possessed and applied to "useful" and "good" purposes, proved emptiness in the end.[2] Wealth, indeed, is nothing if not a means to happiness, yet experience tells us that the pains

---

[1] *Cf.* Schopenhauer, vol. i. 401-402, and *passim*.   [2] ii. 3-11.

endured in striving for it, and the anxiety suffered in preserving it, effectually destroy our capacity for enjoying the bliss which it is supposed to insure, long before misfortune or death snatches it from our grasp.[1]

Vain as pleasure is, in a world of positive evils it is at least a negative good, in that it helps to make us forget the vanity of the days of our life.[2] For this reason, no doubt, it is well-nigh unattainable, the many being deprived of the means, the few of the capacity, of enjoyment.[3]

Passing on to the consideration of wisdom, the Hebrew philosopher finds it equally empty and vain, because subject to the same limitations and characterised by the same drawbacks. It is caviare to the million, and a fresh source of sorrow to the few. Man is tortured with a thirst for knowledge, and yet all the springs at which it might have been allayed are sealed up. Unreal shadows are the objects of human

---

[1] v. 9-16.

[2] Pain, then, for Koheleth, as for a greater than Koheleth, is something positive; pleasure, on the contrary, negative. "We feel pain, but not painlessness; we feel care, but not exemption from it; fear, but not safety. . . . Only pain and privation are perceived as positive and announce themselves; well-being, on the contrary, is merely negative. Hence it is that we are never conscious of the three greatest boons of life—health, youth, and freedom as such, so long as we possess them, but only when we have lost them: for they too are negations. . . . . The hours fly the quicker the pleasanter they are; they drag themselves on the slowlier the more painfully they are passed, because pain, not enjoyment, is the something positive whose presence makes itself felt."—Schopenhauer, ed. Grisebach, ii. 676, 677.

[3] v. 17-vi. 7; iii. 9, 12-13.

intuition, we are denied a glimpse of the underlying reality. For it is unknowable.

Even the little we can know is not inspiring. Take our fellow-men, their ways and works, for instance, and what do we behold? Their own evil-doing, injustice, and violence, drag them down to the level of the brute; and that this is their natural level is obvious, if we bear in mind that the end of men is that of the beasts of the fields,[1] and that the ruling power within them, the mechanism, so to say, of these living and feeling automata is love of life. Consider men at their best— when cultivating such relative "virtues" as industry, zeal, diligence in their crafts and callings, and we find these "good" actions tainted at the very source: love of self and jealousy of others being the determining motives.[2] In any case we see that work is no help to happiness, for it is too evident that toil and moil—even that of the writer himself, who knows full well that he is labouring for a stranger—is but the price we pay, not for real pleasure, but for carking care and poignant grief.[3] Such being the bitter fruits of knowledge, the tree on which they flourish is scarcely worth cultivating.

Wisdom in its ethical aspect, as a rule of right conduct, is unavailing as a weapon to combat the Fate that fights against man. Nay, it is not even a guarantee that we shall be remembered by those who come after us, and whose lot we have striven to render less unbearable than our own. The memory of the dead is buried in their graves,[4] and the wheels of the vast

---

[1] iii. 19-iv. 3.   [2] iv. 4-6.   [3] iv. 7, 8; ii. 18-23.   [4] ii. 13-16.

machine revolve as if they had never lived. For a man's moral worth goes for nothing in the scale against Fate, whose laws operate with crushing regularity, unmodified by his virtues or his crimes.[1] Indeed, if there be any perceptible difference between the lot of the upright and that of the wicked, it is often to the advantage of the latter, who are furthered by their fierce recklessness and borne onwards by ambition.[2] The knowledge of this curious state of things serves but to encourage evil-doers.[3] The obvious conclusion is that instead of fighting against Fate which is unalterable—" I discovered that whatever God doeth is forever "[4]—we should resign ourselves to our lot and draw the practical inference from the fact that life is an evil.

Wisdom in its practical aspect is equally unpromising. In no walk of life is success the meed of merit or victory the unfailing guerdon of heroism.[5] Such wisdom as is within man's reach is often a positive disadvantage in life, owing to the modesty it inspires as pitted against the self-confidence of noisy fools. Besides, should it contrive to build up a stately structure, a small dose of folly, with which all human wisdom is largely alloyed, is capable, in an instant, of undoing the work of years.[6] In a word, the wise man is often worse off than the fool; and in any case, no degree of wisdom can influence the laws of the universe; what happens is foredoomed; a man's life-journey is

---

[1] iii. 1-8, viii. 6-8.   [2] viii. 9-14.   [3] viii. 14, ix. 3.
[4] iii. 14.   [5] ix. 11-12.   [6] ix. 13-18, x. 1.

mapped out beforehand, and it is hopeless to struggle with the Will which is mightier than his own. As we know not what is pre-arranged, we can never find out what will dovetail with our true interests or is really good for man.[1]

---

[1] vi. 8, 10-12.

PRACTICAL WISDOM

HAVING thus cleared the ground in the first part of the treatise, Koheleth proceeds to erect his own modest system in the second. As life offers us no positive good, those who, in spite of this obvious fact, desire it, must make the best of such negative advantages as are within their grasp. Although so far from being a boon, it is an evil, yet it may, he points out, be rendered less irksome by following certain practical rules; and warming to his subject, he winds up with an exhortation to snatch such pleasures as are within reach, for when all accounts have been finally cast up and everything has been said and done, all things will prove vanity, and a grasping of wind.

The ethics open with six metrical strophes composed, so to say, in the minor key, which harmonises with the disheartening conclusions of the foregoing. The theme is the Horatian *Levius fit patientia quicquid corrigere est nefas*. Death is better than life, grief more becoming than mirth, contemplation preferable to desire, deliberation more serviceable than haste.[1] The fleeting joys and the abiding evils of existence,

---

[1] vii. 1–6, vi. 9, vii. 7–9.

are to be taken as we find them, seeing that it is beyond our power to alter the proportions in which they are mixed, even by the practice of virtue and the application of knowledge. Hence even in the cultivation of righteousness the rule, *Ne quid nimis,* is to be implicitly followed: "Be not righteous overmuch, neither make thyself overwise."[1] On the other hand, wisdom is not to be despised, for it hardens us against the strokes of Fate, and renders us insensible to the insults of our fellows.[2] It also teaches us the drawbacks of isolation, the benefits of co-operation, and the advantage of being open to counsel.[3] The basis of all practical wisdom being resignation to the inevitable, obedience to God is better than sacrifices destined to influence His action. What He does, is done for ever, and our efforts are powerless to alter it, or to induce Him to change it.[4] God is far off, unknowable, inaccessible, and man is here upon earth, and such prayers as we feel disposed to offer, had best be short and few; vows too, although to be carried out if once made, serve no good purpose, and are to be avoided. In a word, wild speculations and many words in matters of religion and theology are vain and pernicious.[5] That work and enterprise are beneficial in public and private life is obvious from a study of the results engendered by their opposites.[6] Simple individuals, no less than rulers, may benefit by enterprise and initiative, provided that prudence, by multi-

---

[1] vii. 10, 13-14, 15-18.   [2] vii. 21-22.   [3] iv. 9-16
[4] iii. 14.   [5] v. 1-7.   [6] v. 7-8, x. 16-20.

plying the possibilities of profit, leaves as little as possible to the vagaries of chance.[1] But prudence is especially needed in order to avoid the seductive wiles of woman, against whom one must be ever on one's guard.[2] It also enjoins upon us submission to the political ruler of the day, who possesses the power to enforce his will, and is therefore a living embodiment of the inevitable.[3] In a word, this practical wisdom assumes the form of a careful adjustment of means to the end in all the ups and downs of existence.[4]

After this follows the recommendation of the negative good: the sensuous joys within our reach. Seeing that no man knows what evil is before him, nor what things will happen after him, he cannot go far astray, supposing him to be actuated by a desire to make the best of life, if he tastes in moderation of the pleasures that lie on his path, including those of labour.[5] The young generation should, in an especial manner, take this to heart and pluck the rosebuds while it may, for old age and death are hurriedly approaching to prove by their presence that all is vanity and a grasping of wind.[6]

---

[1] x. 1-3, 6, 4, 5. [2] vii. 26-29. [3] viii. 1-4, x. 2-7.
[4] x. 8-14a, 15. [5] x. 14b, ix. 3-10, xi. 7-10.
[6] xi. 9, xii. 8.

KOHELETH'S PHILOSOPHY OF LIFE

KOHELETH, who agrees with Job in so many other essential points, is likewise at one with him in his views on human knowledge, or, as he terms it, wisdom, which is the source of the highest good within the reach of man. The only light which we have to guide us through the murky mazes of existence, is at best but a miserable taper which serves only to render the eternal darkness painfully visible. "I set my heart to learn wisdom and understanding. And my heart discerned much wisdom and knowledge. . . . . I realised that this also is but a grasping of wind."[1] The scenes it reveals in the moral as well as the material order are of a nature to make us hate existence. "Then I loathed life."[2] Indeed, the so-called moral order which, were it, in theory, what it is asserted to be in truth, might reconcile us to our lot and kindle a spark of hope in the human breast, is but the embodiment of rank immorality. "All things come alike to all indiscriminately; the one fate overtaketh the upright man and the miscreant, the clean and the unclean, him who sacrifices and him who sacrifices not, the just and the sinner."[3] What then is life?

---

[1] i. 17, 16 b.   [2] ii. 17.   [3] ix. 2.

To this question the answer is, in effect, "The shadow of a thing which is not." The sights and sounds of the universe are the only materials upon which the human intellect can work; and they are all alike empty, shadowy, unreal. They are the creation of the mind itself, the web it weaves from its own gossamer substance; and beyond this are nothing. Space and time, or, as Koheleth expresses it, the universe and eternity, were placed in our consciousness from the very first, and are as deceptive as the mirage of the desert.[1] Kant would define them to be functions of the brain. A projection of the organ of human thought, the world is woven of three threads—space, time, and causality—which, being identical with the mind, appear and vanish with it. The one underlying reality, whether we term it God, Nature, or Will, is absolutely unknowable,[2] and everything else is Maya or illusion.

Strange as this doctrine may sound in orthodox ears, it contains, so far, nothing incompatible with Christianity, which teaches that time and space will disappear along with this transitory existence, and that the one eternal and incomprehensible Will is outside the sphere of both and exempt from the operation of the law of cause and effect. The only difference between the two is that Christianity admits the existence of many beings outside the realm of space and time, whereas without space and time multiplicity is inconceivable, impossible.

---

[1] iii. 11.   [2] vii. 24, *cf.* also v. 1.

We cannot hope to know the one reality which is and acts underneath the appearances of which our world is made up, because knowledge is for ever formed, coloured and bounded by time, space, and causation, and all three are unreal. They alone constitute succession and multiplicity, which are therefore only apparent, not existent. We can conceive nothing but what is, was, or will be (and therefore in time), nothing outside ourselves but what is in space, and absolutely nought that is not a cause or an effect. "Far off is that which is, and deep, deep, who can fathom it?"[1]

But we possess insight and understanding enough to enable us to perceive that life is a positive evil, as, indeed, all evil, pain, and suffering are positive; that pleasures are few, and being negative by their nature, merely serve to make us less sensible of the evils of existence; that happiness is a chimæra, birth a curse, death a boon,[2] and absolute nothingness (Nirvāna) the only real good. The hope of improvement, progress, evolution, is a cruel mockery; for the present is but a rehearsal of the past; the future will be a repetition of both;[3] everything that is and will be, was; "what came into being had been long before, and what will be was

---

[1] vii. 24, cf. also viii. 16, 17.

[2] "I appraised the dead who died long since, as happier than the quick who are yet alive; but luckier than both him who is still unborn, who hath not yet witnessed the evil doings under the sun," iv. 2, 3.

[3] In truth, time existing only in the intellect as one of the forms of intuition, there can be neither past nor future, but an everlasting now.

long ago."[1] In a word, what we term progress is but the movement of a vast wheel revolving on its axis everlastingly.

But may we not hope for some better and higher state in the future life beyond the tomb where vice will be punished and virtue rewarded? To this query Koheleth's reply, like that given by Job, is an emphatic negative; and yet the doctrines of the immortality of the soul and of the resurrection were rapidly making headway among the writer's contemporaries. But he descries nothing in the material or moral order of the world to warrant any such belief. What is there in material man that he should be immortal? "Men are an accident, and the beasts are an accident, and the same accident befalleth them all; as these die even so die those, and the selfsame breath have they all, nor is there any preeminence of man above beast; for all is nothingness."[2] Nor can any such flattering hope be grounded upon the moral order, because there are no signs of morality in the conduct of the world. "To righteous men that happeneth which should befall wrong-doers, and that betideth criminals which should fall to the lot of the upright."[3] Nay, "there are just men who perish *through* their righteousness, and there are wicked men who prolong their lives *by means* of their iniquity."[4] Of divine promises and revelations Koheleth—who can hardly claim to be considered a theist, and whose God is Fate, Nature, eternal Will—knows nothing. The

---

[1] iii. 15.   [2] iii. 19.   [3] viii. 14.   [4] vii. 15.

most favourable judgment he can pass upon such theological speculations is far from encouraging: "in the multitude of fancies and prattle there likewise lurketh much vanity."[1] In eternal justice, however, he professes a strong belief, and, like Job, he formulates his faith in the words: "Fear thou God."[2]

To accuse Koheleth of Epicureanism is to take a one-sided view of his philosophy. His conception of life, its pleasures and pains, is as clearly and emphatically expressed as that of the Buddha or of Schopenhauer. He is an uncompromising pessimist, who sees the world as it is. Everything that seems pleasant or profitable is vanity and a grasping of wind; there is nothing positive but pain, nothing real but the eternal Will, which is certainly unknowable and probably unconscious. These truths, however, are not grasped by every one; they are the bitter fruits of that rare knowledge, increase of which is increase of sorrow. The few who taste thereof cling too tenaciously to life, though life be wedded to sorrow and misery, to renounce such deceitful pleasures as are within their reach; and the bulk of mankind revel in the empty joys of living. To all such, Koheleth offers some practical rules of conduct to enable them to make the best of what is to be had; but the gist of his discourse is identical with those of Jesus, of the Buddha, of Schopenhauer—renunciation.

Human pleasures, whatever their origin, are limited in degree by man's capacity for enjoyment; and this is

---
[1] v. 7.   [2] *Ibid.*

an inborn gift, varying in different individuals but unchanging in each. Some dispositions, cheerful and sanguine by nature, tinge even the blackest clouds of misfortune with the rainbow hues of hope; others impart a sombre colour to the most auspicious event, and descry cause for dread in the most complete success, just as the bee sucks honey from the flower which yields only poison to the adder. All joys, although produced by the chemistry of our consciousness, are drawn either from within its inner sphere or from without. The former, known as intellectual pleasures, are relatively lasting because they emanate from what man is; the latter are fleeting because their source is either what he has or what he seems. These are never free from alloy; preceded by the pain of desire, they are accompanied by that of disenchantment and followed by tedium, the worst pain of all; those are exempt from all three, because instead of gratifying passing whims they free the intellect from drudging for the will and afford it momentary glimpses of truth. Wisdom therefore, for Koheleth as for Job, is the greatest boon that can fall to man's lot.[1] And yet the law of compensation, operating here as in all other spheres, sensibility to pain is always proportionate to capacity for intellectual enjoyment.

With regard to the pleasures of possession, seeing that they are often difficult of attainment and always precarious, we must be moderate in their pursuit and make the most of such as fall to our

---

[1] vii. 11, 12.

lot. Contentment here is everything, and contentment is the result of an even balance between desire and fulfilment, the former being always in our power and the latter generally beyond our control. To such happiness as possession can bestow, it is immaterial whether our demands are lowered or our prosperity increased, just as in arithmetic it matters not whether we divide the denominator of a fraction or multiply its numerator by the same number. Therefore, "Better look with the eyes than wander with desire."[1] The golden rule is to keep our wishes within the bounds of moderation, and to adjust them to unfavourable circumstances. The rich man who wants nothing and covets a mere trifle which is beyond his grasp, is supremely wretched, while the poor man who needs much but longs for nothing, is cheerful and contented. But even if wealth were as easily obtained as it is difficult, the law of compensation should deter us from seeking it. "Sweet is the sleep of the toiler, but his wealth suffereth not the rich man to slumber."[2] The only enjoyments common to all men are those which consist in the satisfaction of natural wants; the pleasures which wealth can purchase over and above these are trifling, and more than outweighed by the pain of carking care which it brings in its train. He who labours for this is, therefore, cutting a stick for his own back: "all his days are sorrows and his work grief."[3] "There is no good for man," then—for the common run of mankind who, debarred from intellectual

---

[1] vi. 9.   [2] v. 12.   [3] ii. 23.

enjoyment, yet cling tenaciously to life—"save that he should eat and drink, and make glad his soul in his labour."[1] Health being the condition of all enjoyment, and one of the greatest of earthly boons, care should be taken to preserve it by eating, drinking, labour, and rest, and by moderation in all things. For painlessness, which is positive, is always to be preferred to pleasure, which is negative. It matters little to the strong man that he is otherwise hale and thriving, if he suffer from an excruciating toothache or lumbago. He forgets everything else and thinks only of his misery. The world, then, being a terrestrial hell, they who love it as a dwelling-place cannot do better than try to construct a fireproof abode therein. To hunt for pleasures while exposing oneself to the risk of pain is folly; to escape suffering even at the sacrifice of enjoyments is worldly wisdom. As Aristotle put it, ὁ φρόνιμος τὸ ἄλυπον διώκει, οὐ τὸ ἡδύ. But when all has been said and done, the highest worldly wisdom is but a less harmful species of folly. Existence is an evil, and the sole effective remedy renunciation.

---

[1] ii. 24.

THE SOURCES OF KOHELETH'S PHILOSOPHY

To what extent are these pessimistic doctrines the fruits of Koheleth's own meditations, and how far may they be supposed to reflect the views of the nation which admitted his treatise into its sacred canon? The latter half of this question is answered by the desperate efforts made from the very beginning to correct or dilute his pessimism, and by the grave suspicion with which Jewish doctors continued to regard it, long after the " poison " had been provided with a suitable antidote. Thus the book known as the Wisdom of Solomon, which is accepted as canonical by the Roman Catholic Church, contains a flat contradiction and emphatic condemnation of certain of the propositions laid down by Koheleth, as, for instance, in ch. ii. 1–9, which is obviously a studied refutation of Koheleth's principal thesis, couched mainly in the identical words used by the Preacher himself:

"For they have said, reasoning with themselves, but not right: the time of our life is short and tedious, and in the end of a man there is no remedy, and no man hath been known to have returned from hell.

" For we are born of nothing, and after this we shall be as

if we had not been: for the breath in our nostrils is smoke; and speech a spark to move our hearts.

"Which being put out, our body shall be ashes, and our spirit shall be poured abroad as soft air, and our life shall pass away as the trace of a cloud, and shall be dispersed as a mist, which is driven away by the beams of the sun, and overpowered with the heat thereof.

"And our name in time shall be forgotten, and no man shall have any remembrance of our works.

"For our time is as the passing of a shadow, and there is no going back of our end: for it is fast sealed, and no man returneth.

"Come, therefore, and let us enjoy the good things that are present, and let us speedily use the creatures as in youth.

"Let us fill ourselves with costly wine, and ointments; and let not the flower of the time pass by us.

"Let us crown ourselves with roses before they be withered; let no meadow escape our riot.

"Let none of us go without his part in luxury: let us everywhere leave tokens of joy: for this is our portion, and this our lot."

Although the book was accepted as canonical by generations of Hebrew teachers and was quoted as such by men like Gamaliel, there was always a strong orthodox party among the Jews opposed to its teachings and apprehensive of its influence;[1] nor was it until the year 118 A.D. that the protracted dispute on the subject

---

[1] *Cf.* the epilogue (xii. 9-14), for example, which is one of the most timid and shuffling apologies ever penned.

was at last definitely settled at the Synod which admitted Koheleth into the Canon. It was natural enough that Hebrew theologians should have hesitated to stamp with the seal of orthodoxy a book which the poet Heine calls the Canticles of Scepticism and in which every unbiassed reader will recognise a powerful solvent of the bases of theism ; and the only surprising thing about their attitude is that they should have ever allowed themselves to be persuaded to abandon it.

For Koheleth's pessimistic theory, which has its roots in Secularism, is utterly incompatible with the spirit of Judaism, whichever of its historical phases we may select for comparison. It is grounded upon the rejection of the Messianic expectations and absolute disbelief in the solemn promises of Jahveh Himself. Koheleth cherishes no hope for the individual, his nation, or the human race. The thing that hath been is the same that shall be, and what befell is the same that shall come to pass, and there is no new thing under the sun. . . . .[1] "I surveyed all the works that are wrought under the sun, and behold all was vanity and the grasping of wind."[2] Persians had succeeded Chaldeans ; Cyrus, the Anointed of Jahveh, had come and gone ; Greeks had wrested the hegemony of the East from Persians, but no change had brought surcease of sorrow to the Jews. They were even worse off now than ever before. Jahveh, like Baal of old, was become deaf to His worshippers, many of whom turned away from Him in despair, exclaim-

---

[1] i. 9.   [2] i. 14.

ing, "It is vain to serve God, and what profit is it that we have kept His ordinance?"[1] Koheleth, like Job, never once mentions Jahveh's name, but always alludes to the Eternal Will, which alone is real and unknowable, under the colourless name of Elohim. To say that he believed in a personal God in any sense in which a personal God is essential to a revealed religion, is to misunderstand ideas or to play with words.[2] And Koheleth was a type of a class. Literary men of his day having mockingly asked for the name of the Creator,[3] Koheleth answers that He is inaccessible to men, and that prayer to Him is fruitless.[4] The Jewish aristocracy of his day, desirous of embodying these views in a practical form, sought to abolish once for all the national religion, as a body of belief and practices that had been weighed in the balances and found wanting; while the party that still remained faithful to the law was composed mainly of narrow-minded fanatics, whose wild speculations, long-winded prayers and frequent vows, Koheleth considers deserving objects of derision. He himself held aloof from either camp. He took his stand outside the circle of both, surveying life from the angle of vision of the philosophical citizen of the world. But it would be idle to deny that he had far more in common with the "impious" than with the orthodox.

---

[1] Malachi iii. 14.

[2] Professor Cheyne remarks: "To me, Koheleth is not a theist in any vital sense in his philosophic meditations."—"Job and Solomon," p. 250.   [3] *Cf.* Proverbs xxx. 4.   [4] iii. 14, v. 2.

Thus he scornfully rejects the old doctrine of retribution, and he is never tired of affirming premisses from which the obvious and indeed only conclusion is that the popular conception of a deity who spontaneously created the universe and vigilantly watches over the Hebrew nation, is erroneous, incredible, inconceivable. The Jahveh of olden times, with His grand human passions and petty Jewish prejudices, he simply ignores. He naturally rejects the immortality of the soul—a tenet or theory which was then for the first time beginning to gain ground and to be relied upon as the only means of ultimately righting the wrongs of existence. The fact is that he had no belief in a soul as we understand it. Modern theology regards the indestructible part of man as essentially intelligent, while admitting the fact that intellect is indissolubly associated with the brain, partaking of its vicissitudes during life and vanishing with it apparently for ever at death. Job, Koheleth, and many other writers of the Old Testament hold that if anything of the man persists after the death of the individual, it is unconscious. "The living know at least that they shall die, whereas the dead know not anything at all."[1] In a word, no other philosopher, poet, or proverb-writer of the Old Testament is less orthodox in his beliefs or less Jewish in his sentiments—and Agur alone is more aggressive in his scepticism—than Koheleth.

Much has been written about the sources from which this writer may and even must have drawn his

---

[1] Eccles. ix. 5.

peculiar mixture of pessimism and "Epicureanism," and considerable stress has been laid upon the profound influence which Greek culture is supposed to have exerted upon Jewish thinkers towards the second century B.C., when the moral atmosphere was choked with "the baleful dust of systems and of creeds." The "Epicureanism" of the man who said: "Better is sorrow than laughter," "the heart of the wise is in the mourning house,"[1] hardly needs the hypothesis of a Greek origin to explain it. My own view of the matter, which I put forward with all due diffidence, differs considerably from those which have been heretofore expressed on the subject. I cannot divest myself of the notion that Koheleth was acquainted, and to some extent imbued, with the doctrines of Gautama Buddha, which must have been pretty widely diffused in the civilised world towards the year 205 B.C., when the present treatise was most probably composed.[2]

Buddhism, the only one of the world-religions which, springing from an abstruse system of metaphysics, brought forth such practical fruits as truthfulness, honesty, loving-kindness and universal pity, spread with extraordinary rapidity not only throughout the Indian continent but over the entire civilised world.

---

[1] vii. 3, 4

[2] The view of several of the most authoritative scholars—in which I entirely concur—is that Koheleth was written in Alexandria during the reign of Ptolemy V. (Epiphanes), who came to the throne as a boy under the guardianship of tutors and was alluded to in the verse: "Woe, land, to thee whose king is a child."

Its apostles[1] visited foreign countries, touching and converting by their example the hearts and minds of those who were incapable of weighing their arguments, or unwilling to listen to their exhortations. They introduced a mild, tolerant, humane spirit whithersoever they went, preaching entire equality, practising perfect toleration, founding houses for meditation, erecting hospitals and dispensaries for sick men and beasts, cultivating useful plants and trees, gently suppressing cruelty to animals under any pretext,[2] and generally sowing seeds of sympathy and brotherly love of which history has noticed and described but the final fruits. From the earliest recorded period Indian culture manifested a natural tendency to expand, which was intensified at various times by the comparatively low ebb of civilisation in the adjoining countries. One can readily conceive, therefore, the effects of the strenuous and persevering efforts of one of the most powerful Indian monarchs, Açōka Piyadassī,[3] king of Magadha, to propagate that aspect of his country's civilisation which is indissolubly bound up with the doctrines of the Buddha.

Açōka, grandson of the great king Tshandragupta,

---

[1] Some of them were foreigners resident in India who, after their conversion, preached the new doctrine to their fellow-countrymen. Thus, one of the earliest and most successful missionaries was a Greek, whose Indian name was Dharmarakshita.

[2] Plants, too, were included in their care and profited by their protection.

[3] Açōka is a Sanskrit word, which means " free from care;" and Piyadassī a dialectic form of the Sanskrit word Priyadarsin, which means lovable, amiable. It was applied as an epithet to King Açōka, who reigned from 259-222 B.C.

was the first monarch who openly accepted the tenets and conscientiously practised the precepts of the profoundest religious teacher ever born of woman; and no more eloquent testimony could well be offered to the sincerity of the royal convert than the well-nigh miraculous self-restraint with which he forebore to cajole or coerce those of his subjects whom his arguments failed to convince. Satisfied with the progress of the new religion in his native place, he despatched his son, Mahindo, to introduce it into Ceylon; and so successful were the young prince's missionary efforts that that island became and remains the chief seat of Buddhism to this day. Açōka next turned his attention to foreign countries, in which traders, travellers, emigrants and others had already sparsely sown the seeds of the new faith, and making political power and prestige subservient to zeal for truth and pity for suffering humanity, he induced his allies and their vassals to purchase his friendship by seconding his endeavours to inculcate the philosophic doctrines and engraft the humane practices of Buddhism on their respective subjects. The results he obtained are recorded in his famous inscriptions composed in various Indian dialects and engraven upon rocks all over the continent, from Cabul in the West to Orissa in the East; and among the monarchs whom he there enumerates as having co-operated with him in his apostolic labours, are Antiochus,[1]

---

[1] Antiochus II., called Theos, who was poisoned by his divorced wife Laodikē in 247 B.C. I am aware that some scholars identify the Antiochus here mentioned with Antiochus the Great. Although

Turamaya,[1] Alexander, Magas[2] and Antigenes;[3] into whose hospitable dominions he despatched zealous Buddhist missionaries, empowered to found monasteries, to open dispensaries and hospitals, at his expense, and to preach the saving word to all who cared to hear.

The following literal translation of one of Açōka's inscriptions[4] will help to convey an idea of the nature of his activity as the royal apostle of Buddhism, the Constantine of India: "All over the realms of the god-favoured king, Priyadarsin, and (the realms of those) who (are) his neighbours, such as the Codas, Pandyas, the Prince of the Sâtiyas,[5] the Prince of the Keralas, Tamraparnī, the King of the Javanas, Antiochus, and (among the) others who (are) vassals of the said King Antiochus, everywhere the god-beloved, king, Priyadarsin, caused two kinds of hospitals to be erected: hospitals for men and likewise hospitals for animals.[6] Wherever there were no herbs beneficial to

---

both views make equally for my contention, I fail to see how Açōka, who died in all probability in the year 222 B.C., could have carried on important negotiations with Antiochus the Great, who came to the throne of Syria two years later.

[1] Ptolemy of Egypt, probably Ptolemy Philadelphos, who founded the Museum and Library of Alexandria, and his successor Ptolemy Euergetes (247-221 B.C.).   [2] Magas, king of Cyrene.

[3] The identity of this monarch is uncertain.

[4] The second Edict of Girnar, Khālsi version.

[5] A South Indian people.

[6] Usually a dispensary was opened for the distribution of simples, and a hospital hard by for those who could not move about. The Buddhists were almost as anxious to relieve the physical pain and illness of animals as of human beings.

men or animals, he everywhere gave orders that they should be procured or planted. In like manner, where there were no health-giving roots and fruits, he everywhere commanded that they should be procured or planted. And on the highways he had trees put down and wells dug for the behoof of men and beasts."[1]

History confirms Açōka's testimony and declares him to have been no less successful in sowing the seeds of medicinal plants than those of the "saving doctrine." Buddhism enrolled numerous converts and zealous apostles all over the civilised world, and in Ceylon, Egypt, Bactria, and Persia, the yellow flag floated aloft from the roofs of the monasteries of *Bhikshus*.[2] But its influence, in other ways equally powerful while considerably more subtle, has oftentimes escaped the vigilance of the historian. None of the great religions of ancient or modern times succeeded in escaping its contact, or failed to be improved by its spirit. In the second century B.C. there were flourishing Buddhist communities in inhospitable Bactria, where they maintained a firm footing for nearly a thousand years. A Greek,[3] who wrote about

---

[1] *Cf.* Bühler, "Zeitschrift der deutschen morgenländischen Gesellschaft," Band xxxvii. folg. p. 98.

[2] The monks or real disciples of Buddha who endeavour to attain Nibbāna or Nirvāna. The bulk of the population contents itself with almsgiving and the practice of elementary morality, the reward for which will be a less unhappy existence after death; but not Nirvāna, to which only the perfect can hope to attain.

[3] Alexander Polyhistor, quoted by Cyrillus (*contra Julianum*); *cf.* also Clemens Alexandrinus, *Stromata I.*, p. 339.

the year 80 B.C., and a Chinese pilgrim,[1] who passed through the land in the beginning of the seventh century A.D., allude to them as important elements of the population of the country in their respective ages, and the Buddhist monastery founded in Balkh, the capital of Bactria, in the second century B.C., was become a famous pilgrimage in the days of Hiuen Thsang. The Zoroastrian priests of Erân hated and feared the followers of the strange creed while silently adopting and unconsciously propagating many of its institutions. Several of the Eranian kings incurred the censure involved in the nickname of "idolaters" in consequence of the favour they extended to the preachers of Nirvāna.[2] No religion of antiquity was less favourable to a life of passive contemplation than Zoroastrianism, which defined life as a continuous struggle, and considered virtue as a successful battle with the powers of darkness; and yet little by little Zoroastrian monasteries sprang up by the side of the Fire Temples, and offered a quiet refuge from the turmoil of the world to the pious worshippers of Ahura Mazda.[3]

So saturated were the Eranian populations with the spirit of Buddha—antagonistic though it was to their

---

[1] Hiuen Thsang.

[2] Their names and deeds are preserved in the Persian epic known as the Book of Kings (Firdoosi, Shah-Nameh, *cf.* 1033, v. 4, 1160, v. 2, &c.).

[3] Ormuzd. An instructive instance of the way in which foreign institutions become nationalised in Bactria is afforded by the Buddhist monastery in Balkh, which was at first known by its Indian name, *nava vihāra*, a term that was gradually changed to *naubehar*, which in Persian means "new spring."

own—that the two great Eranian sects,[1] one of which bade fair to become a universal religion,[2] were little else than adaptations of the creed of the Buddha to the needs of a different time and people. Mânî, for instance, prohibited marriage, which was one of the principal duties and holiest acts of a true servant of Ahura Mazda; forbade the killing of animals which, in the case of ants, serpents, gnats, &c., was enjoined by the priests of Zoroaster, and discouraged agriculture lest plants should be destroyed in the process. And the two classes of perfect and imperfect disciples in Mânî's community were copied from those of Buddhism, which divides all believers into two categories: those who sincerely and fervently seek to attain to Nirvāna and are termed Bhikshus, and the Upasakas or laymen who, while holding on to life, practise such virtues as are compatible with this unholy desire.

The Jewish religion, in certain of its phases, reveals in like manner unmistakable traces of the influence of the religion of the Buddha. To take but one instance, the Essenians in Judæa, near the Dead Sea and the Therapeutes in Egypt, practised continence, eschewed all bloody sacrifices, encouraged celibacy, and extreme abstemiousness in eating and drinking. They formed themselves into communities, and lived, after the manner of Buddhist Bhikshus, in monasteries. During the life of Jesus, the Essenians, who lived mostly in cloistered retirement on the shores of the Dead Sea, played no historic rôle; but after the

---

[1] Mânî and Mazdak.   [2] The religion of Mânî.

destruction of Jerusalem, they embraced Christianity in a body, and originated the ascetic movement of the Ebionites, which did not finally subside until it had deposited the germs of monasticism in the Church of Christ.

Koheleth, who lived either in Jerusalem or in Alexandria—more probably in the latter city—about the year 205 B.C., had exceptional opportunities for becoming acquainted with the tenets and precepts of the religion of Buddha. He was evidently a man of an inquiring mind, with a pronounced taste for philosophical speculation; and the social and political conditions of his day were such that a person even of a very incurious disposition would be likely to be brought face to face with the sensational doctrine which was responsible for such amazing innovations as hospitals for men and for animals. Alexandria, the museum and library of which had already been founded, was one of the principal strongholds of non-Indian Buddhists. It is mentioned in the Milindapanho, a Pali work which deals with events that took place in the second century B.C.;[1] it is expressly included by Açōka in the list of cities into which he introduced a knowledge of the "path of duty," and so devoted were its inhabitants to the creed of Sakhya Mouni,[2] that thirty years after Augustine had died at Hippo, thirty thousand Bhikshus set out from Alasadda[3] to annex new countries to the realm of truth.

---

[1] Ed. Trenckner, p. 327.   [2] Buddha.   [3] Alexandria

AGUR, THE AGNOSTIC

AGUR, SON OF YAKEH

EMBEDDED in the collection of the Book of Proverbs [1] is an interesting fragment of the philosophy of a certain "Agur, son of Yakeh, the poet," which for scathing criticism of the theology of his day and sweeping scepticism as to every form of revealed religion, is unmatched by the bitterest irony of Job and the most dogmatic agnosticism of Koheleth. Unfortunately it is no more than a mere fragment, the verses of which are thoughtfully separated from each other by strictures,

---

[1] The Book of Proverbs begins with ten songs on wisdom, which constitute the first part of the work. The second part is made up of distichs, each one of which, complete in itself, embodies a proverbial saying (x. 1-xxii. 16). The third section is composed of the "sayings of the wise men," which are enshrined in tetrastichs or strophes of four lines, among which we find an occasional interpolation by the editor, recognisable by the paternal tone, the words "My son," and the substitution of distichs for tetrastichs. Then comes the appendix containing other proverbial dicta (chap. xxiv. 23-34, chap. vi. 9-19, chap. xxv. 2-10), followed by the proverbs "of Solomon, which the men of Hezekiah copied out" (xxv. 11-xxvii. 22), and wound up with a little poem in praise of rural economy. Chaps. xxviii. and xxix. constitute another collection of proverbs of a more strictly religious character, and then come the sayings of Agur, written in strophes of six lines, the rules for a king and the praise of a good housewife.

protests, and refutations of the baldest and most orthodox kind. Indeed, it is in all probability precisely to the presence of the infallible antidote that we owe the preservation of the deadly poison; and if we may found a conjecture as to the character of the whole work on a comparison of the fragments with what we know generally of the sceptical schools of philosophy prevalent among the Jews of post-Exilian days, we shall feel disposed to hold the seven strophes preserved in our Bibles as that portion of the poem which the compiler considered to be the most innocent because the least startling and revolutionary.

To the thinking of the critics of former times the Proverbs displayed unmistakable traces of the unique and highly finished workmanship of the great and wise king Solomon. At the present day no serious student of the Bible, be he Christian or Rationalist, would raise his voice on behalf of this Jewish tradition which, running counter to well-established facts, is devoid even of the doubtful recommendation of moderate antiquity. A more accurate knowledge of history and a more thorough study of philology have long since made it manifest to all who can lay claim to either, that however weighty may have been Solomon's titles to immortality, they included neither depth of philosophic thought nor finish of literary achievement. And an average supply of plain common-sense enables us to see that even had that extraordinary monarch been a profound thinker or a classic writer, he would hardly have treated future events as accomplished facts without being endowed with further gifts and marked by graver defects which would involve a curious combination of prophecy and folly.

The Proverbs themselves, when properly interrogated, tell a good deal of their own story; sacred and profane history supply the rest. In their present form they were collected and edited by the author of the first six verses of the first chapter, who drew his materials from different sources. The first and most important of these was the so-called "Praise of Wisdom" which, until a comparatively recent period, was erroneously held to be a rounded, homogeneous poem. Professor Bickell conclusively showed that it consists of ten different songs composed in the same metre as the Poem of Job, each chapter being coextensive with one song, except the first chapter, which contains two.[1] The fifth collection, containing the proverbs copied "by the men of Hezekiah," is characterised by the strong national spirit of the writers. Most of the others make frequent mention of God, give a prominent place to religion, and adapt themselves for use as texts for sermons; these, on the contrary, never once mention His name, reflect religion as it was—viz., as only one of the many sides of national existence, and deal mainly with the concrete problems of the everyday life of the struggling people. The other sayings may be aptly described as the pious maxims of a sect; these as the thoughts of a nation. The seventh part of the Book of Proverbs

---

[1] Prov. i. 7-19 and i. 20-33.

contains the remarkable sayings of Agur,[1] which were quite as frequently misunderstood by the Jews of old as by Christians of more recent times, the former heightening the impiety of the author and the latter generously identifying him with the pious and fanatical writer to whose well-meant refutations and protests we owe the preservation of this interesting fragment of ancient Hebrew agnosticism.

---

[1] Chap. xxx.

FORM AND CONTENTS OF THE SAYINGS OF AGUR

It is needless to discuss the condition and the contents of the entire Book of Proverbs, seeing that each one of its component parts has an independent, if somewhat obscure, history of its own. The final compiler and editor, to whom we are indebted for the collection in its present form, undoubtedly found the sweeping scepticism of the poet Agur and the pious protestations of his anonymous adversary, the thesis and the antithesis, inextricably interwoven in the section now known as the thirtieth chapter. He himself apparently identified the two antagonists—the scoffing doubter and the believing Jew; most modern theologians have cheerfully followed his example. The fact would seem to be that the orthodox member of the Jewish community, who thus emphatically objected to aggressive agnosticism, was a man who strictly observed the "Mosaic" Law, and sympathised with the people in their hatred of their heathen masters and their hopes of speedy deliverance by the Messiah; in a word, an individual of the party which later on played an important *rôle* in Palestine under the name of the Pharisees. Possessing a copy of Agur's popular philosophical treatise, this zealous champion undertook to refute the theory before he had ascertained the drift of the sayings in which it was enshrined, or grasped their primary meaning. Thus, in one passage [1] he fancies that the taunts which Agur levelled against omniscient theologians who are well up in the history of everything that is done or left undone in heaven, while amazingly ignorant of the ascertainable facts of earthly science, are really aimed at God; and he seeks to parry the attack accordingly. His numerous and amusing errors are such as characterise the fanaticism that would refute a theory before hearing it unfolded, not those which accompany and betray pious imbecility. Hence it would be unfair to tax him with the utter incoherency of the prayer which our Bibles make him offer up, when warding off the supposed attack upon God: (8) "Feed me with food convenient for me, (9) Lest I be full and deny thee, and say, Who is the Lord? or lest I be poor and steal, and take the name of my God *in vain*." The mistake is the result of the erroneous punctuation of the Hebrew words,[2] which may be literally rendered into English as follows :

> "Feed me with food suitable for me,
> Lest I be sated and deny thee,
> And say, Who is the Lord?
> Or lest I be poor and yield to seduction,
> And sin against the name of my God."

---

[1] Prov. xxx. 4.

[2] The Hebrew text consists of vowelless words. The correct vowels must be ascertained before the meaning of a word or sentence can be definitely established. The vowel points of our Hebrew Bibles are not older than the seventh century A.D., and are fre-

In the ensuing verse the controversialist, full of his own Pharisaic[1] views of politics, and fancying he detects in certain of Agur's words,[2] an apology for the heathen rulers and contempt for the orthodox people of God, inveighs against the traitor who would denounce his fellow-subjects to their common master,[3] and holds him up to universal odium.

One or two other false constructions put upon Agur's sayings by the champion of the "Law of Jahveh," are likewise worthy of attention. In the second sentence, which can be traced back to the proverbial philosophy of the Hindoos, Agur, enumerating the four things that are never satisfied, lays special stress upon two which are, so to say, the beginning and end of all things, the alpha and omega of human philosophy—viz., the grave and the womb;[4] the latter the bait as well as the portal of life, the former the bugbear and the goal of all things living. The idea, no less than the form, is manifestly Indian. Birth and death constitute the axis of existence; the womb is the symbol of the allurement that tempts men to forget their sorrows, to keep the Juggernaut wheel revolving and to supply it with fresh victims to be mangled and crushed into the grave. The lure and the deterrent—love of sensuous pleasure

---

quently erroneous. In the present case the word stealing does not occur in the text, but only the being stolen—viz., seduction, temptation.

[1] I employ the word in its natural, not in its conventional, sense.
[2] Prov. xxx. 21, 22.   [3] *Ibid* xxx. 10.
[4] The word "barren" added in our Bibles (Hebrew '*ozer*, "barrenness") is not only excluded by the metre, but is also wanting in the Septuagint version—conclusive proofs that it is a later interpolation.

and fear of dissolution—are as deceitful as all the other causes of pain and pleasure in this world of appearance. Schopenhauer puts it tersely thus: "As we are decoyed into life by the utterly illusory impulse to voluptuousness, even so are we held fast therein by the fear of death, which is certainly illusory in an equal degree. Both have their immediate source in the Will, which in itself is unconscious."[1]

The only reward which life offers to those who crave it, is suffering and death. The desire of life—the Indian *tanha* or thirst of existence—Agur represents in the form of the beautiful but terrible Ghoul of the desert who has two daughters: birth and death. By means of her fascinating charms she entices the wanderer to her arms, but instead of satiating his soul with the promised joys, she ruthlessly flings him to her two daughters who tear him to pieces and devour him on the spot. Desire is the source of life which in turn is the taproot of all evil and pain; insight into this truth—the knowledge or wisdom lauded by Job and prized by Koheleth—affords the only means of breaking the unholy spell, and escaping from the magic circle.

This ingenious and profound philosophical image was wholly misunderstood by Agur's orthodox adversary, who founds upon the deprecatory allusion to the womb a general accusation of lack of reverence for

---

[1] *Cf.* Schopenhauer, "Die Welt als Wille und Vorstellung," herausg. v. E. Grisebach, ii. p. 585. Grisebach's is the only correct edition of Schopenhauer's works.

AGUR, THE AGNOSTIC

maternity and a specific charge of disrespect for Agur's own mother.[1]

Agur's third saying has been likewise sadly misconstrued by the ancient Pharisaic controversialist and by his faithful modern successors. He enumerates therein four things which to him seem wholly incomprehensible, the fourth and last being the darkest mystery of all: the flying of an eagle in the air, the movement of a serpent—which is devoid of special organs of locomotion—along a rock, the sailing of a ship on the ocean, and "the way of a man with a maid."[2] It is very hard to believe what is nevertheless an undeniable fact, that the bulk of serious commentators classify these as the *trackless* things, whereby, strangely enough, they understand the last of the four in a moral instead of a metaphysical sense. The error is an old one: it was on the strength of this arbitrary and vulgar interpretation that Agur was accused by his Jewish antagonist of a criminal lack of filial piety towards his own father,[3] and threatened with condign punishment, to be inflicted by the eagles that fly so wonderfully in the air;[4] while another scribe, unaware that the mystery of generation could be chosen as the text for a treatise on metaphysics, and firmly convinced that the philosopher was condemning unhallowed relations between the sexes, penned a gloss to make things sufficiently clear which was afterwards removed from the margin to the text where it now figures as the twentieth verse.

---

[1] Prov. xxx. 11. [2] Ib. xxx. 18, 19. [3] Ib. xxx. 11. [4] Ib. xxx. 17.

In truth, Agur gives utterance to a natural sentiment of awe and wonder at the greatest and darkest of all mysteries whose roots lie buried in the depths of the two worlds we conceive of. What could be more awe-inspiring than the instantaneous metamorphosis of pure immaterial will into concrete flesh and blood, throbbing with life hastening to decay, the incarnation in the sphere of appearances of an act of the one being which is not an appearance only, but the denizen of the world of reality? Will is primary, real, enduring; intellect secondary, accidental, fleeting; the one, abiding for ever, is identical in all things; the latter varies in different beings, nay in the same individuals at various times, and perishes with the brain, of which it is a function. Will is devoid of intellect, as intellect is deprived of velleity. We know will through our inner consciousness which has to do exclusively with it and its manifold manifestations; all other things—the world of appearances—we know through what may be termed our outer consciousness.

Now in our self-consciousness we apprehend the fierce, blind, headstrong sexual impulse as the most powerful motion of concentrated will. The act is marked by the spontaneity, impetuosity, and lack of reflection which characterises the agent, will being by nature unenlightened and unconditioned. And yet that which in our inner consciousness is a blind, vehement impulse, appears in our outer consciousness in the form of the most complex living organism we know. Generation, then, is manifestly the point at which the real and the seeming intersect each other.

Birth and death—the inevitable lot of each and every one—would seem to affect the individual only, the race living on without change or decay. This, however, is but the appearance. In reality the individual and the race are one. The blind striving to live, the will that craves existence at all costs, is absolutely the same in both, as complete in the former as in the latter, and the perpetuity of the race is, so to say, but the symbol of the indestructibility of the individual—*i.e.*, of will.

Now this all-important fact is exemplified quite as clearly by the phenomenon of generation as by the process of decay and death. In both we behold the opposition between the appearance and the essence of the being, between the world as it exists in our intellect as representation, and the world as it really is, as will. The act of generation is known to us through two different media: that of the inner consciousness which is taken up with our will and all its movements, and that of our outer consciousness which has to do with impressions received through the senses. Seen through the former medium, the act is the most complete and immediate satisfaction of the will—sensual lust; viewed in the light supplied by the outer consciousness, it appears as the woof of the most intricate texture, the basis of the most complex of living organisms. From this angle of vision, the result is a work of amazing skill, designed with the greatest ingenuity and forethought, and carried out with patient industry and scrupulous care; from that point of view it is the direct outcome of an act which is the negation of plan, forethought, skill, and ingenuity, a blind unreasoning impulse. This contrast or rather opposition between the seeming and the real, this new view of birth and death, this sudden flash of light athwart the impenetrable darkness, is what provokes the wonder of this scoffing sceptic.[1]

In the fourth saying, Agur mentions, among the persons whom the earth cannot endure, 'a low-bred fellow who is set to rule over others, and a fool when he acquires a competency and becomes independent. The anonymous Pharisee, who keeps a vigilant watch for doctrinal slips and political backslidings and frequently finds them where they are not, descries in the first of the four unbearable things a proof that Agur was a Sadducee and an aristocrat who would rather obey a monarch who is "every inch a king" —even though he be a heathen—than a native clodhopper who should climb up to the throne on the backs of a poor deluded people and grind them down in the sacred name of liberty and independence. Agur is therefore duly reprimanded and classed with the shameless oppressors of the multitude and the devourers of the substance of the poor,[2] as the Sadducees generally were by their Pharisaic opponents.

The sentence that follows, enumerating the things "which are little upon the earth,[3] is not from the pen of our philosopher, but a harmless passage inserted subsequently as a *pendant* to the four things which

---

[1] *Cf.* Schopenhauer, "Die Welt als Wille und Vorstellung," vol. ii. p. 583 fol.; also vol. i. pp. 424-426; and Bickell, "Wiener Zeitschrift für Kunde des Morgenlandes," 1891.

[2] Prov. xxx. 19.   [3] *Ib.* xxx. 24-28.

"are comely in going." The main considerations that point to this conclusion and warrant us in ascribing the verses to a different author are these: all the other "numerical sayings" which are admittedly the work of Agur, contain first of all the number three and in the parallel verse four,[1] whereas this sentence speaks of four only. Again, all Agur's proverbs are in the form of strophes of six lines each; but this passage consists of five distichs. Lastly, it is a manifest digression, leads nowhither, and, what is still more important, has no point, as all Agur's sayings have.[2]

The final sentence of this interesting fragment needs no elaborate explanation: it contains the pith of Agur's practical philosophy in the form of an exhortation to renounce honour, glory, the esteem of men, &c., if we possess legitimate claims to such, and still more if we have none; the acquisition of peace and quiet is cheap at the price of obscurity; freedom from care and worry and from the evils they bring in their train, being of infinitely greater value than the chance and even the certainty of so-called "positive" enjoyments.

---

[1] For example, Prov. xxx. 15:
"There are three things that are never satisfied,
Yea, four things say not, 'It is enough!'"

[2] *Cf.* Bickell, "Wiener Zeitschrift für Kunde des Morgenlandes," 1891.

DATE OF COMPOSITION

THE sayings of Agur cannot possibly be assigned to a date later than the close of third century B.C. The ground for this statement is contained in the circumstance that Jesus Sirach found the Book of Proverbs in existence, with all its component parts and in its present shape, about the year 200 B.C. He mentions a collection of proverbial sayings when alluding to Solomon and his proverbs. Jesus Sirach's canon—if we can apply this technical term to the series of scriptures in vogue in his day—comprised the books contained in our Bibles from Genesis to Kings, further Isaiah, Jeremiah, Ezechiel, the twelve Minor Prophets, Psalms, Proverbs, and Job. Moreover, it is no longer open to doubt that the arrangement of the various parts of the Book of Proverbs which he read was identical with that of ours. For the last part of this Book contains an alphabetical poem in praise of a good housewife,[1] and Jesus Sirach concluded his own work with a similar poem upon wisdom, in which he imitated this alphabetical order. It is obvious, therefore, that Proverbs in their present form could not have been compiled later than

---

[1] Prov. xxxi. 10–31.

the date of Jesus Sirach's work (about 200 B.C.). This conclusion is borne out by the circumstance that the final editor of Proverbs in his introduction,[1] mentions the Words of the Wise, which occur in chapters xxii. 17–xxiv., and "their dark sayings," or riddles, by which he obviously means the sentences of Agur. For Proverbs and for Agur's fragment, therefore, the latest date is the beginning of the second century B.C. Chapter xxx., in which, on the one hand, Agur develops very advanced philosophical views, some of them of Indian origin, and, on the other, his anonymous antagonist breathes the narrow, fanatic spirit so thoroughly characteristic of the later "Mosaic" Law, is among the very latest portions of Proverbs. For it is in the highest degree probable that the sayings of Agur are of a much later date even than the promulgation of the Priests' Code;[2] and the circumstance that the anonymous stickler for strict orthodoxy already begins to accentuate the political and religious opposition between the two great parties known as Pharisees and Sadducees, as well as other grounds of a different order, disposes me to assign the fragment of Agur to the third century B.C. This conclusion would be borne out by the influence upon Agur's scepticism of comparatively recent foreign speculation. Some of his sayings have an unmistakable Indian ring about them. A few are even directly traceable to the philosophical sentences of the Hindoos. The enumeration of the four in-

---

[1] Prov. i. 6.   [2] 444 B.C.

satiable things, for instance, is but a slight modification of the Indian proverb in the Hitopadeça which runs: "Fire is not satiated with fuel; nor the sea with streams; nor death with all beings; nor a fair-eyed woman with men."[1] Still more striking and suggestive is the correspondence between the desire of life, personified in Agur's fragment by the beautiful Ghoul, and the thirst of existence denoted by the Buddha and his countrymen as *tanha*—the root of all evil and suffering. "Through thirst for existence (*tanha*)," the Buddha is reported to have said to his disciples, "arises a craving for life; through this, being; through being, birth; through birth are produced age and death, care and misery, suffering, wretchedness and despair. Such is the origin of the world. . . . . By means of the total annihilation of this thirst for existence (*tanha*) the destruction of the craving for life is compassed; through the destruction of the craving for life, the uprooting of being is effected; through the uprooting of being, the annihilation of birth is brought about; by means of the annihilation of birth the abolition of age and death, of care and misery, of suffering, wretchedness and despair is accomplished. In this wise takes place the annihilation of this sum of suffering."[2] The same doctrine is laid down by the last accredited of the Buddha's disciples, Sariputto: "What, brethren, is the source of suffering?" he is

---

[1] *Cf.* Hitopadeça, book ii. fable vi.; ed. Max Müller, vol. ii. p. 38.
[2] Samyuttaka-Nikāyo, vol. ii. chap. xliv. p. 12; *cf.* Neumann "Buddhistiche Anthologie," Leiden, 1892, pp. 161-162

reported to have said. " It is that desire (*tanha*) which leads from new birth to new birth, which is accompanied by joy and passion, which delights now here, now there; it is the sexual instinct, the impulse towards existence, the craving for development. That, brethren, is what is termed the source of suffering."[1]

---

[1] Majjhima-Nikāyo; cf. Neumann, op. cit., p. 25.

AGUR'S PHILOSOPHY

OF the three Hebrew thinkers of the Old Testament who ventured to sift and weigh the evidence on which the religious beliefs of their contemporaries were based, Agur was probably the most daring and dangerous. He appealed directly to the people, and set up a simple standard of criticism which could be effectively employed by all. Hence, no doubt, the paucity of the fragments of his writings which have come down to us and the consequent difficulty of constructing therewith a complete and coherent system of philosophy. To what extent he assented to the theories and approved the practices which constitute the positive elements of the Buddha's religion, is open to discussion; but that he was a confirmed sceptic as regards the fundamental doctrines of Jewish theology, and that his speculations received their impulse and direction from Indian philosophy, are facts which can no longer be called in question.

To the theologians of his day he shows no mercy; for their dogmas of retribution, Messianism, &c., he evinces no respect; nay, he denies all divine revelation and strips the deity itself of every vestige of an attribute. Proud of their precise and exhaustive knowledge of the mysteries of God's nature, the doctors of the Jewish community had drawn up comprehensive formulas for all His methods of dealing with mankind, and anathematised those who ventured to cast doubts upon their accuracy.

> "Whatever sceptic could inquire for,
> For every why they had a wherefore,"

the unanswerable tone of which lay necessarily and exclusively in the implicit and tenacious faith of the hearer. Now, faith may be governed by conditions widely different from those that regulate scientific knowledge, but if its object be something that lies beyond the ken of the human intellect it must be based either upon a supernatural intuition accorded to the individual or upon a divine revelation vouchsafed to all. In the former case it cannot be embodied in a religious dogma; in the latter it cannot—or should not—be accepted without thorough discussion and due verification of the alleged historical fact of the divine message.

This is the gist of Agur's reasoning against the all-wise theologians of the Jewish Church.

These sapient specialists, whose intellects were nurtured upon the highest and most abstruse speculations and who could readily account for all the movements of the Deity with a wealth of detail surpassing that of a French police *dossier*, were utterly and notoriously ignorant of the rudimentary laws of science which every inquisitive mind might learn and every educated man could verify. Now, as truth is one, Agur reasoned, how comes it that the persons who thus lay claim to a thorough knowledge of the more difficult, are absolutely ignorant of the more simple? Whence, in a word, did they obtain their perfect acquaintance with the mysteries of the divine nature and the mechanism of the universe, the elementary laws of which are yet unknown to them? Surely not from any source accessible to all; for Agur, possessing equally favourable opportunities for observation and quite as keen an interest in the subject, not only failed to make any similar discoveries, but even to find any confirmation of theirs. For this he sarcastically accounts by admitting that he must be considerably more stupid than the common run of mankind, in fact, that he is wholly devoid of human understanding—a confession which he evidently expects every reasonable man to repeat after him to those who assert that crass ignorance of fundamental facts is an aid to the highest kind of knowledge.

> "I have worried myself about God, and succeeded not,
> For I am more stupid than other men,
> And in me there is no human understanding:
> Neither have I learned wisdom,
> So that I might comprehend the science of sacred things."

Still he is a very docile disciple, and, having failed to make any discoveries of his own, would gladly accept those of a qualified master—of one who endeavours to know before setting out to teach and who prefaces his account of the wonders of the unseen world by pointing out the bridge over which he passed thither, from this. But does such a genuine teacher exist?

"Who has ascended into heaven and come down again?
 Who can gather the wind in his fists?
 Who can bind the waters in a garment?
 Who can grasp all the ends of the earth?
 Such an one would I question about God: 'What is his name?
 And what the name of his sons, if thou knowest it?'"

And if even specialists do not fulfil these conditions, are we not forced to conclude that their so-called knowledge is a fraud and its subject-matter unknowable?

Agur's views of right conduct—if we may judge by the general tenour of his fragmentary sayings and by the principle embodied in his sixth and last sentence, in which he rejects as a motive for action "a high hope for a low heaven"—are marked by the essential characteristics of true morality. An action performed for the sake of any recompense, human or divine, transitory or eternal, is egotistic by its nature, and therefore not moral; and the difference between the man who, in his unregenerate days, cut his neighbours' throats in order to enjoy their property, and after his conversion gave all his goods to feed the poor, in order to enjoy eternal happiness in heaven, is more interesting to the legislator than to the moralist. But, were it otherwise, Agur holds that, even from a purely practical point of view, all the honours and rewards which mankind can bestow upon their greatest benefactor would be too dearly purchased by a ruffled temper; in other words, mere freedom from positive pain is a greater boon than the highest pleasure purchased at the price of a little suffering.

Agur's politics gave as much offence to the priests as his theology. Like most original thinkers, he is a believer in the aristocracy of talent, and he makes no secret of his preference of a hereditary nobility to those upstarts from the ranks of the people who possess no intellectual gifts to recommend them. For the former have at least training and heredity to guide them, whereas the latter are devoid even of these recommendations. These views furnished the grounds for the charge of Sadducceism preferred against him by his adversary.

To what extent Indian thought, and in particular the metaphysics and ethics of Buddhism, influenced Agur's religious speculations, it is impossible to do more than conjecture. Personally I am disposed to think that he was well acquainted and indeed thoroughly imbued with the teachings of the Indian reformer. In the third century B.C., as already pointed out, the spread of the new religion through Bactria, Persia, Egypt, and Asia Minor was rapid. Moreover, the turn taken by the speculations of cultured Hebrews of that epoch was precisely such as we should expect to find, if it stood to Buddhistic preaching in the relation of effect to cause. The scepticism of the philosophers of the Old Testament, not excepting that of Agur who may aptly be termed the Hebrew Voltaire, was not wholly destructive. Its sweeping negations in the spheres of metaphysics and theology were amply compensated for—if one can speak of compensation in such a connection—by the positive, humane, and wise maxims it lays down in the domain of ethics. And the corner-stone of the morality of all three—Job, Koheleth, and Agur—would seem to be virtually identical with that formulated in the Indian aphorism:

> "Alone the doer doth the deed; alone he tastes the fruit it brings;
> Alone he wanders through life's maze; alone redeems himself from being."

Buddhistic influence in the case of Agur, therefore, is all the more probable that it admirably dovetails with all the circumstances of time and place known to us, even on the supposition, which I am myself inclined to favour, that Agur lived and wrote in Palestine. This probability is greatly enhanced by the striking affinity between the Buddhist conception of revealed religions, of professional priests and of practical wisdom, and that enshrined in the few verses of Agur which we possess. It is raised to a degree akin to certainty by the actual occurrence of Indian images, similes, and even concrete aphorisms in the short fragment of seven strophes preserved to us in the Book of Proverbs.

THE POEM OF JOB

TRANSLATION OF THE RESTORED TEXT

PROLOGUE

CHAP. I. A.V.]

1 *There was a man in the land of Uz, whose name was Job; and that man was perfect and upright, and one that feared God, and eschewed evil.*

2 *And there were born unto him seven sons and three daughters.*

3 *His substance also was seven thousand sheep, and three thousand camels, and five hundred yoke of oxen, and five hundred she asses, and a very great household; so that this man was the greatest of all the men of the east.*

4 *And his sons went and feasted* in their *houses, every one his day; and sent and called for their three sisters to eat and to drink with them.*

5 *And it was so, when the days of* their *feasting were gone about, that Job sent and sanctified them, and rose up early in the morning, and offered burnt offerings* according *to the number of them all: for Job said, It may be that my sons have sinned, and cursed God in their hearts. Thus did Job continually.*

6 ¶ *Now there was a day when the sons of God came to present themselves before the Lord, and Satan came also among them.*

7 *And the Lord said unto Satan, Whence comest thou? Then Satan answered the Lord, and said, From going to and fro in the earth and from walking up and down in it.*

8 *And the Lord said unto Satan, Hast thou considered my servant Job, that* there *is none like him in the earth, a perfect and an upright man, one that feareth God, and escheweth evil?*

9 *Then Satan answered the Lord, and said, Doth Job fear God for nought?*

10 *Hast not thou made an hedge about him, and about his house, and about all that he hath on every side? thou hast blessed the work of his hands, and his substance is increased in the land.*

11 *But put forth thine hand now, and touch all that he hath, and he will curse thee to thy face.*

12 *And the Lord said unto Satan, Behold, all that he hath* is *in thy power; only upon himself put not forth thine hand. So Satan went forth from the presence of the Lord.*

13 ¶ *And there was a day when his sons and his daughters were eating and drinking wine in their eldest brother's house:*

14 *And there came a messenger unto Job, and said, The oxen were plowing, and the asses were feeding beside them:*

15 *And the Sabeans fell* upon them, *and took them away; yea, they have slain the servants with the edge of the sword; and I only am escaped alone to tell thee.*

16 *While he* was *yet speaking, there came also another, and said, The fire of God is fallen from heaven, and hath burned up the sheep, and the servants, and consumed them; and I only am escaped alone to tell thee.*

17 *While he* was *yet speaking, there came also another, and said, The Chaldeans made out three bands, and fell upon the camels, and have carried them away, yea, and slain the servants with the edge of the sword: and I only am escaped alone to tell thee.*

18 *While he* was *yet speaking, there came also another, and*

said, Thy sons and thy daughters were eating and drinking wine in their eldest brother's house:

19 *And, behold, there came a great wind from the wilderness, and smote the four corners of the house, and it fell upon the young men, and they are dead; and I only am escaped alone to tell thee.*

20 *Then Job arose, and rent his mantle, and shaved his head, and fell down upon the ground and worshipped,*

21 *And said, Naked came I out of my mother's womb, and naked shall I return thither: the Lord gave, and the Lord hath taken away; blessed be the name of the Lord.*

22 *In all this Job sinned not, nor charged God foolishly.*

CHAP. II. A.V.]

1 *Again there was a day when the sons of God came to present themselves before the Lord, and Satan came also among them to present himself before the Lord.*

2 *And the Lord said unto Satan, From whence comest thou? And Satan answered the Lord, and said, From going to and fro in the earth, and from walking up and down in it.*

3 *And the Lord said unto Satan, Hast thou considered my servant Job, that* there is *none like him in the earth, a perfect and an upright man, one that feareth God, and escheweth evil? and still he holdeth fast his integrity, although thou movedst me against him, to destroy him without cause.*

4 *And Satan answered the Lord, and said, Skin for skin, yea, all that a man hath will he give for his life.*

5 *But put forth thine hand now, and touch his bone and his flesh, and he will curse thee to thy face.*

6 *And the Lord said unto Satan, Behold he* is *in thine hand: but save his life.*

7 ¶ *So went Satan forth from the presence of the Lord,*

and smote Job with sore boils from the sole of his foot unto his crown.

8 *And he took him a potsherd to scrape himself withal; and he sat down among the ashes.*

9 ¶ *Then said his wife unto him, Dost thou still retain thine integrity? curse God, and die.*

10 *But he said unto her, Thou speakest as one of the foolish women speaketh. What! shall we receive good at the hand of God, and shall we not receive evil? In all this did not Job sin with his lips.*

11 ¶ *Now when Job's three friends heard of all this evil that was come upon him, they came every one from his own place; Eliphaz the Temanite, and Bildad the Shuhite, and Zophar the Naamathite: for they had made an appointment together to come to mourn with him and to comfort him.*

12 *And when they lifted up their eyes afar off, and knew him not, they lifted up their voice, and wept; and they rent every one his mantle, and sprinkled dust upon their heads toward heaven.*

13 *So they sat down with him upon the ground seven days and seven nights, and none spake a word unto him: for they saw that his grief was very great.*

CHAP. III. A.V.]

1 *After this opened Job his mouth, and cursed his day.*
2 *And Job spake, and said:*

I

JOB:

Would the day had perished wherein I was born,
And the night which said: behold, a man child!
Would that God on high had not called for it,
And that light had not shone upon it!

II

Would that darkness and gloom had claimed it for their own;
Would that clouds had hovered over it;
Would it never had been joined to the days of the year,
Nor entered into the number of the months!

III

Would that that night had been barren,
And that rejoicing had not come therein;
That they had cursed it who curse the days,[1]
That the stars of its twilight had waxed dim!

IV

Would it had yearned for light but found none,
Nor beheld the eye-lids of the morning dawn!
For it closed not the door of my mother's womb,
Nor hid sorrow from mine eyes.

---

[1] *I.e.*, the magicians by means of incantations.

V

Why died I not straight from the womb?
Why, having come out of the belly, did I not expire?
Why did the knees meet me?
And why the breasts, that I might suck?

VI

For then should I have lain still and been quiet,
I should have slept and now had been at rest,
With the kings and counsellors of the earth,
Who built desolate places for themselves.

VII

Or with princes, once rich in gold,
Who filled their houses with silver,
I should be as being not, as an hidden untimely birth,
Like infants which never saw the light!

VIII

There the wicked cease from troubling,
And there the weary be at rest;
There the prisoners repose together,
Nor hear the taskmaster's voice.

IX

Why gives he light to the afflicted,
And life unto the bitter in soul,
Who yearn for death, but it cometh not,
And dig for it more than for buried treasures?

X

Hail to the man who hath found a grave!
Then only hath God "hedged him in."[1]
For sighing is become my bread,
And my crying is unto me as water.

XI

For the thing I dreaded cometh upon me,
And that I trembled at befalleth me.
I am not in safety, neither have I rest;
Nor quiet, but trouble cometh alway.

XII

ELIPHAZ:

Lo, thou hast instructed many,
Thy words have upholden him that was stumbling.
Now hath thine own turn come,
And thou thyself art worried and troubled.

XIII

Was not the fear of God thy confidence?
And the uprightness of thy ways thy hope?
Bethink, I pray thee, who ever perished guiltless?
Or where were the righteous cut off?

---

[1] Allusion to the Satan's remark in the Prologue, chap. i. 10: "Hast not thou made an hedge about him, and about his house, and about all that he hath on every side?"

XIV

I saw them punished that plough iniquity,
And them that sow sorrow reap the same;
By the blast of God they perish,
And by the breath of his nostrils are they consumed.[1]

XV

Now a word was wafted unto me by stealth,[2]
And mine ear received the whisper thereof;
In thoughts from the visions of the night,
When deep sleep falleth upon man.

XVI

Fear came upon me and trembling,
Which made all my bones to shake.
Then a spectre sped before my face;
The hair of my flesh bristled up.

XVII

It stood, but I could not discern its form.
I heard a gentle voice:—

---

[1] The strophe which follows in Prof. Bickell's text I consider a later insertion, and have therefore struck it out. It runs thus:

> "The roaring of the lion, and the voice of the fierce lion,
> And the teeth of the young lions are broken;
> The old lion perisheth for lack of prey,
> And the stout lion's whelps are scattered abroad."

[2] The prophetic vision which Eliphaz now describes is relied

"Shall a mortal be more just than God?
Shall a man be more pure than his maker?

XVIII

Behold, in his servants he puts no trust,—
Nay, his angels[1] he chargeth with folly;—
How much less in the dwellers in houses of clay,
Whose foundations are down in the dust.

XIX

Between dawn and evening they are destroyed:
They perish and no man recketh.
Is not their tent-pole torn up?[2]
And bereft of wisdom, they die."

XX

Call now, if so be any will answer thee;
And to which of the angels wilt thou turn?
For his own wrath killeth the foolish man,
And envy slayeth the silly one.

---

upon by him as the sanction for his whole discourse. To his seeming, it is a direct revelation from God.

[1] The sons of God, sons of the Elohim. *Cf.* Genesis vi. 4. There is no analogy between these sons of God and the angels or saints of Christianity. *Cf.* also Prof. Cheyne, "Job and Solomon," p. 81; Baudissin, Studien, II.

[2] The human body is likened to a tent of which the tent-pole is the breath of life; this gone, all that remains is the natural prey of the elements.

XXI

His children are far from safety;
They are crushed, and there is none to save them.
The hungry eateth up their harvest,
And the thirsty swilleth their milk.

XXII

For affliction springeth not out of the dust,
Nor doth sorrow sprout up from the ground;—
For man is born unto trouble,
Even as the sparks fly upward.

XXIII

But I would seek unto God,
And unto God would I commit my cause,
Who doth great things and unfathomable,
Marvellous things without number.

XXIV

He giveth rain unto the earth,
And sendeth waters upon the fields;
To set up on high those that be low,
That they who mourn may be helped to victory.

XXV

He catcheth the wise in their own craftiness,
And the counsel of the cunning is thwarted;
Wherefore they encounter darkness in the daytime,
And at noonday grope as in the night.

XXVI

The poor he delivereth from the sword of their mouth,
And the needy out of the hand of the mighty;
Thus the miserable man obtaineth hope,
And iniquity stoppeth her mouth.

XXVII

Happy is the man whom God correcteth;
Therefore spurn not thou the chastening of the Almighty:
For he maketh sore and bindeth up;
He smiteth, and his hands make whole.

XXVIII

He shall deliver thee in six troubles,
Yea in seven there shall no evil touch thee:—
In famine he shall redeem thee from death,
And in war from the power of the sword.

XXIX

Thou shalt be hid from the scourge of the tongue,[1]
Neither shalt thou fear misfortune when it cometh;
At destruction and famine thou shalt laugh,
Nor shalt dread the beasts of the earth.

XXX

For thy tent shall abide in peace,
And thou shalt visit thy dwelling and miss nought therein;

---

[1] Calumny.

Thou shalt likewise know that thy seed will be great,
And thine offspring as the grass of the earth.

XXXI

Thou shalt go down to thy grave in the fulness of thy days,
Ripe as a shock of corn brought home in its season.
Lo, this have we found out, so it is!
This we have heard, and take it thou to heart.

XXXII

JOB:

Oh that my "wrath" were thoroughly weighed,
And my woe laid against it in the balances!
For it would prove heavier than the sands of the sea;
Therefore are my words wild.

XXXIII

For the arrows of the Almighty are within me;
My spirit drinketh in the venom thereof.
The terrors of God move against me,
He useth me like to an enemy.

XXXIV

Doth the wild ass bray when he hath grass?
Or loweth the ox over his fodder?
Would one eat things insipid without salt?
Is there taste in the white of raw eggs?

XXXV

Oh that I might have my request,
And that God would grant me the thing I long for!
Even that it would please him to destroy me,
That he would let go his hand and cut me off!

XXXVI

Then should I yet have comfort,
Yea, I would exult in my relentless pain.
For that, at least, would be my due from God,
Since I have never withstood the words of the Holy One.

XXXVII

What is my strength that I should hope?
And what mine end that I should be patient?
Is my strength the strength of stones?
Or is my flesh of brass?

XXXVIII

Am I not utterly bereft of help?
And is not rescue driven wholly away from me?
Is not pity the duty of the friend,
Who, else, turneth away from the fear of God?

XXXIX

My brethren have disappointed me as a torrent,
They pass away as a stream of brooks,
Which were blackish by reason of the ice,
Wherein the snow hideth itself.

XL

The caravans of Tema sought for them,
The companies of Sheba hoped for them.
But when the sun warmed them they vanished;
When it waxed hot they were consumed from their place.

XLI

Did I say: Bestow aught upon me?
Or give a bribe for me of your substance?
Or deliver me from the enemy's hand?
Or redeem me from the hand of the mighty?

XLII

Teach me and I will hold my tongue;
And cause me to discern wherein I have erred.
How cutting are your "righteous" words!
But what doth your arguing reprove?

XLIII

Do ye imagine to rebuke words?
But the words of the desperate are spoken to the wind.
Will ye even assail me, the blameless one?
And harrow up your friend?

XLIV

But now vouchsafe to turn unto me,
For surely I will not lie to your face.
I pray you, return; let no wrong be done.
Return, for justice abideth still within me.

XLV

Is there iniquity in my tongue?
Cannot my palate discern misfortunes?
Hath not man warfare upon earth?
And are not his days like to those of an hireling?

XLVI

As a slave panting for the shade, and finding it not,
As an hireling awaiting the wage for his work,
So to me months of sorrow are allotted,
And wearisome nights are appointed to me.

XLVII

Lying down I exclaim: When shall I arise?
And I toss from side to side till the dawning of the day:[1]
My flesh is clothed with worms and clods of dust,
My skin grows rigid and breaks up again.

---

[1] Allusion to his sufferings at night from elephantiasis. This terrible malady, which was first described by Rhazes, in the ninth century, under the name of *dá-l-fil* ("disease of the elephant"), was for a long time erroneously believed to be confined to Arabia. As a matter of fact, it is found in an endemic state in all warm countries, and sporadically even in Europe. In tropical and sub-tropical lands it progresses with alarming rapidity. Every new crisis is preceded by a shivering sensation and violent fever, frequently accompanied with headache, delirium, and nervous and gastric suffering. A violent attack of this kind may last seven or eight days. The seat of the disease is generally the foot or the reproductive organs. In the former case the foot swells to a monstrous size, instep, toes and heel and ankle all merging in one dense mass that reminds one of the foot of an elephant.

XLVIII

My days are swifter than a weaver's shuttle,
And have come to an end without hope;[1]
Remember, I pray, that my life is wind,
That mine eye shall see good no more.

XLIX

As the cloud is dispelled and vanisheth away,
So he that goes down to the grave shall not come up again;
He shall never return to his house,
Neither shall his place know him any more.

L

I too will not restrain my mouth,
I will speak out in the bitterness of my soul.
Am I a sea or a sea-monster,[2]
That thou settest a watch over me?

LI

When I say: "My bed shall comfort me,
My couch shall ease my complaint;"
Then thou scarest me with dreams,
And terrifiest me with visions.

---

[1] Job feels that death is nigh.

[2] Allusion to an ocean myth. A watch had to be set upon the movements of the monsters of the sea and the firmament.

LII

Then my soul would have chosen strangling,
And death by my own resolve:
But I spurned it, for I shall not live for ever;
Let me be, for my days are a breath.

LIII

What is man that thou shouldst magnify him?
And that thou shouldst set thine heart upon him?
That thou shouldst visit him every morning,
And try him every moment?[1]

LIV

Why wilt thou not look away from me?
Nor leave me in peace while there is breath in my throat?
Why hast thou set me up as a butt,
So that I am become a target for thee?

LV

Why dost thou not rather pardon my misdeed,
And take away mine iniquity?
For now I must lay myself down in the dust,
And thou shalt seek me, but I shall not be.

---

[1] The irony of these words addressed by Job to Jehovah would be deemed blasphemous in a poet like Byron or Shelley. As a matter of fact, they constitute a parody of Psalm viii. 5, as Prof. Cheyne has already pointed out ("Job and Solomon," p. 22).

LVI

BILDAD:

How long wilt thou utter these things,
And shall the words of thy mouth be like a storm wind?
Doth God pervert judgment?
Or doth the Almighty corrupt justice?

LVII

If thou wouldst seek unto God,
And make thy supplication to the Almighty,
He would hear thy prayer,
And restore the house of thy blamelessness.

LVIII

For inquire, I pray thee, of the bygone age,
And give heed to the search of the forefathers;
Shall they not teach thee,
And utter words out of their heart?

LIX

Can the papyrus grow without marsh?
Can the Nile-reed shoot up without water?
Whilst still in its greenness uncut,
It withereth before any herb.

LX

Such is the end of all that forget God,
And even thus shall the hope of the impious perish,

Whose hope is as gossamer threads,
And whose trust is as a spider's web.

LXI

For he leans upon his house,
And has a firm footing to which he cleaves;
He is green in the glow of the sun,
And his branch shooteth forth in his garden.

LXII

But his roots are entangled in a heap of stones,
And rocky soil keeps hold upon him;
It destroyeth him from his place,
Then that denying him saith: "I have not seen thee."

LXIII

Behold, this is the "joy" of his lot,
And out of the dust shall others grow.
Lo! God will not cast out a perfect man,
Neither will he take evil-doers by the hand.

LXIV

He will yet fill thy mouth with laughing
And thy lips with rejoicing.
They that hate thee shall be clothed with shame,
And the tent of the wicked shall disappear.

LXV

JOB:

I know it is so of a truth;
For how should man be in the right against God?
If he long to contend with him,
He cannot answer him one of a thousand.

LXVI

Wise is he in heart and mighty in strength:
Who could venture against him and remain safe?—
Against him who moveth mountains and knoweth not
That he hath overturned them in his anger.

LXVII

He shaketh the earth out of her place,
And the inhabitants thereof quake with fear;
He commandeth the sun and it riseth not,
And he sealeth up the stars.[1]

LXVIII

He alone spreadeth out the heavens,
And treadeth upon the heights of the sea;
He doth great things past finding out,
Yea, and wonders without number.[2]

---

[1] The firmament, being a solid mass, has paths cut out along which the stars move in their courses, just as there are channels made for the clouds and rain.

[2] This entire speech is ironical.

LXIX

Lo, he glideth by me and I see him not;
And he passeth on, but I perceive him not.
Behold, he taketh away, and who can hinder him?
Who will say unto him: "What dost thou?"

LXX

God will not withdraw his anger;
The very helpers of the sea-dragon[1] crouch under him.
How much less shall I answer him,
And choose out my words to argue with him?

LXXI

I must make supplication unto his judgment,
Who doth not answer me, though I am righteous,
Who would sweep me away with a tempest,
And multiply my wounds without cause!

LXXII

He will not suffer me to take my breath,
But filleth me with bitterness.
If strength be aught, lo, he is strong,
And if judgment, who shall arraign him?

LXXIII

Though I were just, my own mouth would condemn me:
Though I were faultless, he would make me crooked.

---

[1] Allusion to a myth.

Faultless I am, I set life at naught ;
I spurn my being, therefore I speak out.

LXXIV

He destroyeth the upright and the wicked,
When his scourge slayeth at unawares.
He scoffeth at the trial of the innocent :
The earth is given into the hand of the wicked.

LXXV

My days are swifter than a runner :
They flee away, they have seen no good ;
They glide along like papyrus-boats,
Like the eagle swooping upon its prey.

LXXVI

If I say : " I will forget my complaint,
I will gladden my face and be cheerful ; "
Then I shudder at all my sorrows :
I know thou wilt not hold me guiltless.

LXXVII

If I washed myself with snow,
And cleansed my hands with lye,
Thou wouldst plunge me in the ditch,
So that mine own garments would loathe me.

LXXVIII

Would he were like unto myself, that I might answer
    him,
That we might come together in judgment!
Would there were an umpire between us,
Who might lay his hand upon us both!

LXXIX

Let him but withdraw from me his rod,
And let not dread of him terrify me;
Then would I speak and not fear him,
For before myself I am not so.[1]

LXXX

My soul is aweary of life,
I will let loose my complaint against God;
I will say unto God: Hold me not guilty;
Show me wherefore thou contendest with me.

LXXXI

Is it meet that thou shouldst oppress,
Shouldst thrust aside the work of thine hands?
Seest thou as man seeth?
Are thy days as the days of mortals?

---

[1] In the light of my own conscience I am not an evil-doer.

LXXXII

For thou inquirest after mine iniquity,
And searchest after my sin,
Though thou knowest that I am not wicked,
And that there is none who can deliver out of thine hand.

LXXXIII

Thine hand hath made and fashioned me,
And now hast thou turned to destroy me;
Remember, I pray thee, that thou hast formed me as clay:
And now wilt thou grind me to dust again?

LXXXIV

Didst thou not pour me out as milk,
And curdle me like cheese?
Hast thou not clothed me with skin and flesh?
And knitted me with bones and sinews?

LXXXV

Thou enduedst me with life and grace;
And thy care hath cherished my spirit.
And yet these things hadst thou hid in thy heart!
I know that this was in thee!

LXXXVI

Had I sinned, thou wouldst have watched me,
Nor wouldst have acquitted me of my wrongdoing.
Had I been wicked, woe unto me!
And though righteous, I dare not to lift up my head

LXXXVII

As a lion thou huntest me, who am soaked in misery,
And ever showest thyself marvellous [1] against me!
While I live, thou smitest me ever anew,
And lettest thy wrath wax great against me.

LXXXVIII

Wherefore, then, didst thou bring me out of the womb?
Would I had then given up the ghost, and no eye had seen me!
I should now be as though I had never been;
I had been borne from the womb to the grave.

LXXXIX

Are not the days of my life but few,
So that he might let me be, while I take heart a little
Before I depart whence I shall not return,
To the land of darkness and of gloom?

XC

ZOPHAR:

Shall the multitude of words be left unanswered?
And shall the prattler [2] be deemed in the right?
Should men hold their peace at thy babbling?
And when thou jeerest, shall none make thee ashamed?

---

[1] Ironical. [2] *Lit.*, the man of lips.

XCI

But oh that God would speak,
And open his lips against thee,
And that he would show thee the secrets of wisdom
That they are as marvels to the understanding!

XCII

It[1] is high as heaven; what canst thou do?
Deeper than hell; what canst thou know?
The measure thereof is longer than the earth,
And broader than the ocean.

XCIII

For he knoweth men of deceit;
He seeth wickedness and needeth not to gauge it.
Thus[2] the empty man gets understanding,
And the wild-ass' colt is born anew as man.

XCIV

If thou make ready thine heart,
And stretch out thine hands towards him,
Then shalt thou lift up thy face,
And in time of affliction be fearless.

---

[1] Wisdom.

[2] *I.e.*, God's wisdom enables him to discern the deceit of those who appear just, and the punishment which he deals out to them makes the result of his knowledge visible to the dullest comprehension.

XCV

For then shalt thou forget thy misery,
And remember it as waters that have passed away;
The darkness shall be as morning,
And thine age shall be brighter than the noonday.

XCVI

Thou shalt be secure because there is hope,
Thou shalt look around and take thy rest in safety;
Thou shalt lie down and none shall startle thee,
Yea, many shall make suit unto thee.

XCVII

But the eyes of the wicked shall fail,
And refuge shall vanish from before them;
Their hope shall be the giving up of the ghost;
For with him is wisdom and might.

XCVIII

JOB:

No doubt but ye are clever people,
And wisdom shall die with you;
I too have understanding as well as ye;
Just, upright is my way.

XCIX

He that is at ease scorneth the judgments of Shaddai.[1]
His foot stands firm in the time of trial.

---

[1] A name for God.

The tents of robbers prosper,
And they that provoke God are secure.

C

But ask, I beseech you, the beasts,
And the fowls of the air, and they shall tell thee;
Or speak to the earth and it shall teach thee,
And the fishes of the sea shall declare unto thee.

CI

Is not the soul of every living thing in his hand,
And the breath of all mankind?
Doth not the ear try words
As the mouth tasteth its meat?

CII

For there is no wisdom with the aged,[1]
Nor understanding in length of days;
With him is wisdom and strength;
He hath counsel and understanding.

CIII

Behold he breaketh down and it cannot be builded anew:
He shutteth up a man, and who can open to him?

---

[1] The current versions of the Bible make Job say the contrary: "With the ancient *is* wisdom; and in length of days understanding" (Job xii. 12, Authorised Version). *Cf. ante,* "Interpolations," pp. 53-54.

Lo, he withholdeth the waters and they dry up,
He letteth them loose and they overwhelm the earth.

CIV

With him is strength and wisdom,
The erring one and his error are his,
Who leadeth away counsellors barefoot,
And rendereth the judges fools.

CV

He bringeth back kings into their mausoleums,
And overthroweth the nobles;
He withdraweth the speech of the trusty,
And taketh away the understanding of the aged.

CVI

He poureth scorn upon princes,
And looseth the girdle of the strong;
He discovereth deep things out of darkness,
And bringeth gloom unto light.

CVII

He stealeth the heart of the chiefs of the earth,
And maketh them wander in a pathless wilderness
So that they grope in the dark without light,
And stagger to and fro like a drunken man.

CVIII

Lo, mine eye hath seen all this,
Mine ear hath heard and understood it.
What ye know, the same do I know also;
I am nowise inferior to you.

CIX

But now I would speak to the Almighty,
And I long to argue with God;
For ye are weavers of lies,
Ye all are patchers of inanities.

CX

Oh that ye would all of you hold your peace,
And that should stand you in wisdom's stead!
Hear, I beseech you, the reasoning of my mouth,
And hearken to the pleadings of my lips!

CXI

Will ye discourse wickedly for God?
And utter lies on his behalf?[1]
Will ye accept his person by dint of trickery?
Will ye contend for God with deception?

---

[1] *I.e.*, Will ye persist in maintaining that God rewards the good and punishes the wicked (as Zophar has just done, strophe xcvii.) in spite of the fact that ye know it is untrue?

CXII

Were it well for you should he search you out?
Can ye dupe him as ye dupe men?
Will he not surely rebuke you,
If ye secretly[1] accept his person?

CXIII

Shall not his majesty, then, make you afraid?
And his dread seize hold of you?
Will not your adages become as ashes,
Your arguments even as bulwarks of clay?

CXIV

Hold your peace that I may speak,
And let come upon me what will!
I shall take my life in my teeth,
And put my soul in mine hand.

CXV

Lo, let him kill me, I cherish hope no more,
Only I will justify my way before his face.
This too will aid my triumph,
That no wicked one dares appear in his sight.

---

[1] *I.e.*, not on grounds obvious to all, but because your own particular lot is satisfactory.

CXVI

Behold now, I have ordered my cause ;
I know that I shall be justified.
Who is he that will plead with me?
Only do not two things unto me!

CXVII

Withdraw thine hand from me,
And let not dread of thee make me afraid.
Then call thou and I will answer,
Or let me speak and answer thou unto me.

CXVIII

How many are mine iniquities?
Make me to know my misdeeds.
Wherefore hidest thou thy face,
And holdest me for thine enemy?

CXIX

Wilt thou scare a leaf driven to and fro?
And wilt thou pursue the dry stubble?
That thou writest down bitter things against me,
And imputest to me the errors of my youth.

CXX

Thou observest all my paths,
And puttest my feet into the stocks,

Thy chain weigheth heavy upon me,
And cutteth into my feet.[1]

CXXI

Man that is born of a woman,
Poor in days and rich in trouble;
He cometh forth like a flower and fadeth,
He fleeth as a shadow and abideth not.

CXXII

And upon such an one dost thou open thine eyes!
And him thou bringest into judgment with thee!
Though he is gnawed as a rotten thing,
As a garment that is moth-eaten.

CXXIII

If his days are determined upon earth,
If the number of his months are with thee;
Look then away from him that he may rest,
Till he shall accomplish his day, as an hireling.

CXXIV

For there is a future for the tree,
And hope remaineth to the palm:
Cut down, it will sprout again,
And its tender branch will not cease.

---

[1] Compare this with the extraordinary verse in our Authorised Version: "Thou settest a print upon the heels of my feet"! (Job . 27).

CXXV

Though its roots wax old in the earth
And its stock lie buried in mould,
Yet through vapour of water will it bud,
And bring forth boughs like a plant.

CXXVI

But man dieth, and lieth outstretched;
He giveth up the ghost, where is he then?
He lieth down and riseth not up;
Till heaven be no more he shall not awake.

CXXVII

Oh that thou wouldst hide me in the grave!
That thou wouldst secrete me till thy wrath be passed!
That thou wouldst appoint me a set time and remember me!
If so be man could die and yet live on!

CXXVIII

All the days of my warfare I then would wait,
Till my relief should come;
Thou wouldst call and I would answer thee,
Thou wouldst yearn after the work of thine hands.

CXXIX

But now thou renumberest my steps,
Thou dost not forgive my failing;
Thou sealest my transgressions in a bag,
And thou still keepest adding to my guilt.

CXXX

ELIPHAZ:

Should a wise man utter empty knowledge,
And fill his belly with the east wind?
Should he reason with bootless prattle?
Or with speeches that profit him nothing?

CXXXI

Yea, thou makest void the fear of God,
And weakenest respect before him;
For thine own iniquity instructeth thy mouth,
And thou choosest the tongue of the crafty.

CXXXII

Art thou the first man born?
Or wast thou made before the hills?
Wast thou heard in the council of God?
And hast thou drawn wisdom unto thyself?

CXXXIII

What knowest thou that we know not?
What understandest thou which is not in us?
Doth the solace of God not suffice unto thee,
And a word to thee whispered softly?

CXXXIV

Why doth thine heart carry thee away,
And what do thine eyes wink at,

That thou turnest thy spirit against God,
And lettest go such words from thy mouth?

CXXXV

Behold he putteth no trust in his saints;
Yea, the heavens are not clean in his sight;
How much less the foul and corrupt one,—
Man, who lappeth up wickedness like water.

CXXXVI

What the wise announce unto us,
Their fathers did not withhold it from them;
Unto them alone the land was given,
And no stranger passed among them.[1]

CXXXVII

The wicked man travaileth all his days with pain,
And few are the years appointed to the oppressor:
A sound of dread is in his ears:
In prosperity the destroyer shall overtake him.

CXXXVIII

He has no hope of return out of darkness,
And he is waited for by the sword.

---

[1] This is one of the very few passages in the Poem which throw light upon the date of its composition.

The day of gloom shall terrify him,
Distress and anguish shall fasten upon him.

CXXXIX

For he stretched out his arm against God,
And girded himself against the Almighty:
Rushing upon him with a stiff neck,
Guarded by the thick bosses of his buckler.

CXL

The glow shall dry up his branches,
And his blossom shall be snapped by the storm-wind.
Let him not trust in vanity—he is deluded,
For his barter[1] shall prove worthless.

CXLI

His offshoot shall wither before his time,
And his branch shall not be green;
He shall shake off his unripe grape, like the vine,
And shall shed his flower like the olive.

CXLII

For the tribe of the wicked shall be barren,
And fire shall consume the tents of bribery:
They conceive mischief, and bring forth disaster,
And their belly breeds abortion.

---

[1] *I.e.*, the object for which he bartered righteousness.

CXLIII

JOB:

Many such things have I heard before.
Stinging comforters are ye all!
Shall idle words have an end?
What pricks thee that thou answerest?

CXLIV

I, too, could discourse as ye do,
If your souls were in my soul's stead.
I would inspirit you with my mouth,
Nor would I grudge the moving of my lips.

CXLV

But he hath so jaded me that I am benumbed;
His whole host[1] hath seized me.
His wrath hackles me and pursues me,
He gnashes upon me with his teeth.

CXLVI

The arrows of his myriads have stricken me,
He whets his sword, fixing his eyes upon me.
They smite me on the cheek outrageously,
They mass themselves together against me.

---

[1] Host of evils which has attacked me from all sides.

CXLVII

God hath turned me over to the ungodly,
And delivered me into the hands of the wicked.
I was at ease, but he clove me asunder,
He throttled me and shook me to pieces.

CXLVIII

He sets me up for his target;
His archers compass me round about;
He rives my reins asunder, and spareth not,
He poureth out my gall upon the ground.

CXLIX

With breach upon breach he breaketh me,
He rusheth upon me like a warrior;
Sackcloth and ashes cover me,
And my horn has been laid in the dust.

CL

My face is aglow with weeping
And darkness abides on my eyelids;
Though on my hands there is no evil,
And my prayer is pure!

CLI

Oh earth! cover not thou my blood!
And let my cry find no resting-place!

Even now behold my witness is in heaven,
And my voucher is on high.

CLII

My friends laugh me wantonly to scorn;
Mine eye poureth tears unto God.
Let him adjudge between man and God,
And between man and his fellow.

CLIII

Soon will the wailing-women come,
And I go the way I shall not return.
My spirit is spent, the grave is ready for me
Truly I am scoffed at.

CLIV

Hold still my pledge in thy keeping,
Who then will be my voucher?[1]
He yielded his friends as a prey,
And the eyes of his children must shrivel up.

CLV

He hath made me a by-word of the peoples,
And they spit into my face.
My eye is dim by dint of sorrow,
And all my members are as a shadow.

---

[1] Ironical.

CLVI

At this the upright are appalled,
And the just bridles up against the impious.
But the righteous holds on his way,
And the clean-handed waxeth ever stronger.

CLVII

But as for you all—do ye return,
For I discern not one wise man among you.
My days, my thoughts have passed away;
My heart's desires are cut asunder.

CLVIII

If I still hope, it is for my house—the tomb.
I have made my bed in the darkness.
I have said unto the grave, "My Mother,"
And to the maggot, "Sister mine."

CLIX

And my hope—where is it now?
My bliss—who shall behold it?[1]
They go down to the bars of the pit,
When our rest together is in the dust.

---

[1] An allusion to the promises made by the friends on the part of God that Job would, if he repented and asked for pardon, recover his former prosperity.

CLX

BILDAD:

When wilt thou make an end of words?
Reflect, and then let us speak!
Wherefore are we counted as beasts?
Deemed silenced in thy sight?

CLXI

Shall the earth be deserted for thy sake?
And shall the rock be removed from its place?
Still the light of the wicked shall be douted,
And the spark of his fire shall not twinkle.

CLXII

The light in his tent shall be dark;
And his taper above him shall be put out.
The steps of his strength shall be straitened,
And his own design shall ruin him.

CLXIII

For he is tangled in the net by his own feet,
And he walketh upon a snare.
The slings shall catch him;
Many terrors rage menacingly round him.

CLXIV

Hunger shall dog his footsteps;
Misery and ruin stand ready by his side:

The limbs of his body[1] shall be gnawed,
Devoured by the firstborn of death.[2]

CLXV

He shall be dragged out from his stronghold,
And he shall be brought to the king of terrors;[3]
The memory of him shall vanish from the earth,
He shall be driven from light into darkness.

CLXVI

He shall have nor son nor offspring among his people,
And he shall have no name above the ground;
None shall survive in his dwellings;
Strangers shall dwell in his tent.

CLXVII

They of the west are astonied at him,
And those of the east stand aghast:
Such are the dwellings of the wicked,
And this his place who knoweth not God.

CLXVIII

JOB:

How long will ye harrow my soul,
And crush me with words?

---

[1] *Lit.*, the pieces of his skin.
[2] Probably an allusion to elephantiasis.
[3] The personification of death.

Already ten times have ye insulted me,
Ever incensing me anew.

CLXIX

If indeed ye will glorify yourselves above me,
And prove me guilty of blasphemy;
Know, then, that God hath wronged me,
And hath compassed me round with his net!

CLXX

Lo, I cry out against violence, but I am not heard;
I cry aloud, but there is no judgment.
He hath fenced up my way that I cannot pass;
And he hath set darkness in my paths.

CLXXI

He hath stripped me of my glory,
And taken the crown from my head.
On all sides hath he ruined me, and I am undone;
And mine hope hath he felled like a tree.

CLXXII

He hath kindled against me his wrath,
And looketh on me as one of his foes.
His troops throng together on my way,
And encamp round about my tent.

CLXXIII

He hath put my brethren far from me,
And mine acquaintance are estranged from me;
My kinsfolk stay away from me,
And my bosom friends have forgotten me.

CLXXIV

They that dwell in my house, and my maids,
As an alien am I in their eyes.
I call my servant, and he giveth me no answer,
I must supplicate unto him with my mouth.

CLXXV

My breath is irksome to my wife,
And my entreaty to the children of my body.
Yea, mere lads despise me:
When I arise, they talk about me.

CLXXVI

All my cherished friends abhor me,
And they whom I loved are turned against me;
My skin cleaveth to my bones,
And my teeth are falling out.

---

[1] Either "the sons of the womb which has borne me," as in iii. 10, or else "my own children," the poet forgetting that in the prologue they are described as having been killed.

CLXXVII

Have pity, have pity on me, O my friends!
For the hand of God hath smitten me.
Why do ye persecute me like God,
And are not satiated with my flesh?

CLXXVIII

Oh would but that my words,
Oh would that they were written down!
Consigned to writing for ever,
Or engraven upon a rock!

CLXXIX

But I know that my avenger liveth,
Though it be at the[1] end upon my dust;
My witness will avenge these things,
And a curse alight upon mine enemies.

CLXXX

My reins within me are consumed,
Because you say: "How we shall persecute him!"
Fear, for yourselves, the sword,
For "wrath overtaketh iniquities."

---

[1] *I.e.*, when it is too late.

CLXXXI

ZOPHAR:

It is not thus that my thoughts inspire me,
Nor is this the eternal law that I have known.[1]
No; the triumph of the wicked is shortlived,
And the joy of the ungodly is but for a twinkling.

CLXXXII

Though his height tower aloft to the heavens,
And his head reach up to the clouds,
Yet shall he perish for ever like dung,
They who have seen him shall ask: "Where is he?"

CLXXXIII

He flitteth like a dream and shall not be found,
Yea, he shall be chased away as a vision of the night;
His hands having crushed the needy,
Must restore the substance, and he cannot help it.

CLXXXIV

He hath swallowed down riches and shall disgorge them anew;
They shall be driven out of his belly.
He hath sucked in the poison of asps,
The viper's tongue shall slay him.

---

[1] Zophar discerns perfect moral order in the world.

CLXXXV

He shall not gaze upon the rivers,
The brooks of honey and milk;
He must restore the gain and shall not swallow it,
His lucre shall be as sand which he cannot chew.

CLXXXVI

For the poor he had crushed and forsaken;
Had robbed an house but shall not build it up.
Nought had escaped from his greed,
Therefore shall his wealth not endure.

CLXXXVII

In the fulness of his abundance he shall be in straits,
Every hand of the wretched shall come upon him:
He[1] shall cast the fury of his wrath upon him,
And shall rain down upon him terrors.

CLXXXVIII

When he fleeth from the iron weapon,
Then the arrow of steel shall transfix him;
He draweth, and it cometh out of his back,
And the glittering steel out of his gall.

---

[1] God.

CLXXXIX

Terrors will trample upon him,
All darkness is hid in store for him;
A fire not kindled[1] shall consume him,
What remaineth in his tent shall be devoured thereby.

CXC

The heavens reveal his iniquity,
And the earth riseth up against him:
This is the wicked man's portion from God,
And the heritage appointed him by Elohim.

CXCI

JOB:

Hearken diligently to my speech,
And let that stand me in your comfort's stead!
Suffer me that I may speak;
And after that I have spoken, mock on!

CXCII

As for me, is my complaint to men?
And how should not my spirit be impatient?
Look upon me, and tremble,
And lay your hand upon your mouth![2]

---

[1] *I.e.*, by man.   [2] *I.e.*, be silent.

CXCIII

Even when I remember, I am dismayed,
And trembling taketh hold on my flesh.
Wherefore do the wicked live?
Become old, yea, wax mighty in strength?

CXCIV

Their houses are safe from fear,
Neither is the rod of God upon them;
Their bull genders and faileth not,
Their cow casteth not her calf.

CXCV

Their seed is established in their sight,
And their offspring before their eyes;
They send forth their little ones like a flock,
And their children skip about.

CXCVI

They take down the timbrel and the harp,
And delight in the sound of the bagpipe;
They while away their days in bliss,
And in a twinkling go down to the grave.[1]

---

[1] Job's ideal of a happy death was identical with that of Julius Cæsar—the most sudden and least foreseen.

CXCVII

And yet they say unto God: "Depart from us,
We desire not the knowledge of thy ways."
Yet hold they not happiness in their own hands?
Is he not heedless of the counsel of the wicked?

CXCVIII

How oft is "the lamp of evil-doers put out"?
And how often doth "ruin" overwhelm them?
How oft are they as stubble before the wind,
And as chaff that the storm carries away?

CXCIX

Ye say, "God hoards punishment for the[1] children."
Let him rather requite the wicked himself that he may
    feel it!
His own eyes should behold his downfall
And he himself should drain the Almighty's wrath!

CC

If his sons are honoured,[2] he will not know it,
And if dishonoured, he will not perceive it.
Only in his own flesh doth he feel pain,
And for his own soul will he lament.

---

[1] Literally, "his."   [2] *I.e.*, after his death.

CCI

Is the wicked taught understanding by God?
And does he judge the man of blood?
Nay, he[1] filleth his milk vessels with milk,
And supplieth his bones with marrow.

CCII

But the guiltless dies with embittered soul,
And hath never enjoyed a pleasure;
Then they alike lie down in the dust,
And the worms shall cover them both.

CCIII

Behold I know your thoughts,
And the plots which ye wrongfully weave against me.
And how will ye comfort me in vain,
Since of your answers nought but falsehood remains?

CCIV

ELIPHAZ:

Can a man be profitable unto God?
Only unto himself is the wise man serviceable.
Is it a boon to the Almighty that thou art righteous?
Or is it gain to him that thou makest thy way perfect?

---

[1] *I.e.*, God.

CCV

Will he reprove thee for thy fear of him?
Will he enter with thee into judgment for that?
Is not rather thy wickedness great?
Are not thine iniquities numberless?

CCVI

For thou hast taken a pledge from thy brother for nought,
And stripped the naked of their clothing;
Thou hast not given water to the weary to drink,
And hast withholden bread from the hungry.

CCVII

But as for the mighty man, he held the land,
And the honoured man dwelt in it.
Thou hast sent widows away empty,
And the arms of the fatherless have been broken.

CCVIII

Therefore snares are round about thee,
And sudden fear troubleth thee;
Thy light hath become darkness, thou canst not see,
And a flood of waters covereth thee.

CCIX

Doth not God look down from the height of heaven,
And crush the mighty for that they are grown haughty,

Which say unto God : " Depart from us,"
And " What can the Almighty do against us ? "

CCX

And he forsooth " shall fill their houses with goods,"
And " be heedless of the counsel of the wicked " !
No ; the righteous shall look on and be glad,
And the innocent shall laugh them to scorn.

CCXI

Befriend now thyself with him, and thou shalt be safe,
Thereby shall good come unto thee.
Receive, I pray thee, instruction from his mouth,
And treasure up his words in thine heart.

CCXII

If thou turnest to God and humblest thyself,
If thou remove iniquity from thy tent,
Then shalt thou have delight in the Almighty,
And shalt lift up thy face unto God.

CCXIII

Thou shalt pray unto him and he shall hear thee,
And thou shalt pay thy vows ;
If thou purpose a thing, it shall prosper unto thee,
And a light shall shine upon thy ways.

CCXIV

JOB:

Oh, I know it already: I myself am to blame for my
    misery,[1]
And his hand is heavy upon me by reason of my groaning!
Oh that I knew where I might find him,
That I might come even unto his seat!

CCXV

I would plead my cause before him,
And fill my mouth with arguments;
I would fain know the words which he could answer me,
And learn what he would say unto me.

CCXVI

Will he plead against me with his almighty power?
If not, then not even he would prevail against me.
For a righteous one would dispute with him;
So should I be delivered for ever from my judge.

CCXVII

Behold I go forward, but he is not there,
And backward, but I cannot perceive him.
For he knoweth the way that I have chosen:
If he would try me, I should come forth as gold.

---

[1] Ironical.

CCXVIII

My foot has held his steps,
His way have I kept and swerved not;
I have not gone back from the precept of his lips,
I have hid the words of his mouth in my bosom.

CCXIX

But he is bent upon one thing and who can turn him away?
And what his soul desireth even that he doeth.
Therefore am I troubled before his face;
When I consider, I am afraid of him.

CCXX

God hath crushed my heart,
And the Almighty hath terrified me.
For I am annihilated because of the darkness,
And gloom enwrappeth my face.

CCXXI

Why do the times of judgment depend upon the Almighty,
And yet they who know him do not see his days?[1]
The wicked remove the landmarks;
They rob flocks and lead them to pasture.

---

[1] If there be a God who rules the world, punishes evil, and rewards good, how comes it that we descry no signs of such just retribution?

CCXXII

They drive away the ass of the fatherless,
The widow's ox they seize for a pledge;
They turn the needy out of the way,
All the poor of the earth have to hide themselves.[1]

CCXXIII

Lo, these things mine ear hath heard,
Mine eye hath seen them, and so it is.[2]
And if it be not so now, who will make me a liar,
And render my speech meaningless?

CCXXIV

BILDAD:

Dominion and fear are with him,
Who maketh peace in his high places.
Is there any number to his armies?
And upon whom doth his light not arise?

---

[1] About seven strophes in the same quasi-impious strain, characterising the real reign of Jehovah upon earth as distinguished from the optimistic delineations of Job's friends, are lost. The verses that have taken their place in our manuscripts are portions of a different work, which has no relation whatever to our poem. They are not even in the same metre as Job, but contain strophes of three lines only.

[2] Conjecture of Professor Bickell; these two lines are not found in the MSS.

CCXXV

By his power the sea groweth calm,
And by his understanding he smiteth the sea-dragon.
By his breath the heavens become splendour;
His hand hath pierced the bolt-serpent.

CCXXVI

But the thunder of his power,
Who understands its working?
And how can man be deemed just before God,
And how can he be clean who is born of a woman?

CCXXVII

Behold, even the moon shineth not,
Yea, the stars are not pure in his sight;
How much less man, the worm;
And the son of man, the maggot!

CCXXVIII

JOB:

How hast thou helped him that is without power?
How upholdest thou the arm that hath no strength?
To whom hast thou uttered words?
And whose spirit went out from thee?

CCXXIX

As God liveth who hath taken away my right,
And the Almighty who hath made my soul bitter,

Never shall my lips confess untruth,
Nor my tongue give utterance to falsehood!

CCXXX

Far be it from me to agree with you!
Till I die I will not yield up my integrity!
My righteousness I hold fast and will not let it go,
My heart doth not censure any one of my days.

CCXXXI

I will teach you about the hand of God,
The counsel of the Almighty will I not conceal.
Behold, all ye yourselves have seen it.[1]
Why then do ye utter such empty things?

CCXXXII

For there is a mine for silver,
And a place for gold where they fine it;
Iron is taken out of the dust,
And copper is smolten out of the stone.

CCXXXIII

He that hovers far from man hath made an end to gloom,[2]
He turneth the mountains upside down.

---

[1] I will judge ye out of your own mouths. Ye maintained, all of you, that the principles on which the world is governed are absolutely unintelligible. How then can ye reason as if the moral order were based upon retribution, and from my sufferings infer my sins?

[2] The miner who descends into the abyss of the earth, and carries a lamp.

He cutteth out stulms among the rocks,
And the thing that is hid he bringeth forth to light.

CCXXXIV

But wisdom—whence shall it come?
And where is the place of understanding?
It is hid from the eyes of all living,
Our ears alone have heard thereof.[1]

CCXXXV

God understandeth its way,
And he knoweth its dwelling-place;
For he looketh to the ends of the earth,
And seeth under the entire heaven.

CCXXXVI

When he made the weight for the winds,
And weighed the waters by measure,
Then did he see and declare it,
He prepared it, yea, and searched it out.

CCXXXVII

Then he said unto man, "Desist!
Worry not about things too high for thee.

---

[1] Wisdom is here identified with God, of whom we know nothing and have only vaguely heard from those who knew less, *i.e.*, former generations, for whom Job has scant respect.

Behold, fear of me, that is wisdom,
And to depart from evil, that is understanding."

CCXXXVIII

ZOPHAR:

May the lot of the wicked befall mine enemy,
And that of the ungodly him who riseth up against me!
For what can be the hope of the iniquitous,
When God cutteth his soul away?

CCXXXIX

Will God hear his cry,
When trouble overtaketh him?
Will he delight himself in the Almighty?
Will he always call upon God?

CCXL

If his children be multiplied, it is for the sword,
And his offspring shall not be sated with bread;
They that survive him shall be buried in death,
And their widows shall not weep.

CCXLI

Though he heap up silver as the dust
And store up raiment as the clay,
He may indeed prepare it, but the just shall put it on,
And the guiltless shall divide the silver.

CCXLII

He buildeth his house as a spider;
Rich shall he lie down, but rich he shall not remain.
Terrors take hold on him like waters;
A tempest sweepeth him away in the night.

CCXLIII

JOB:

Oh that I were as in months gone by,
As in the days when God preserved me;
When his lamp shined upon my head,
And when I walked by his light through darkness!

CCXLIV

For then I moved in sunshine,
While God was familiar with my tent;
While I washed my steps in cream,
And the rock poured me out rivers of oil.

CCXLV

When I went to the gate at the city,[1]
When I prepared my seat on the public place,
Then the young men, seeing me, hid themselves,
And the aged arose and remained standing.

---

[1] To mete out justice.

THE POEM OF JOB

CCXLVI

Princes desisted from talking,
And laid their hands upon their mouths;
For the ear heard me and blessed,
The eye saw me and bore me witness.

CCXLVII

For I delivered the poor that cried aloud,
And the orphan and him that had none to help him;
The blessing of him that was perishing came upon me,
And I gladdened the heart of the widow.

CCXLVIII

I put on righteousness and it clothed me;
My judgment was as a robe and a diadem.
I became eyes to the blind,
And I was feet unto the lame.

CCXLIX

I was a father to the poor,
And the cause which I knew not I searched out;
And I brake the grinders of the wicked,
And plucked the spoil out of his teeth.

CCL

Unto me men gave ear and waited,
And kept silence at my counsel.

After my words they spake not again,
And my speech fell upon them as a shower.

CCLI

But now they laugh me to scorn,
Shepherd boys approach me with insolence,
Whose fathers I would not have deigned
To set with the dogs of my flock.

CCLII

Yea, what booted me the strength of their hands?
Pity upon them was thrown away.
They were children of fools, yea, men of no name,
They were driven forth from the land.

CCLIII

And now I am become the song of these!
Yea, I am become their byword!
They loathe me, they flee far from me,
And withhold not spittle from my face.

CCLIV

For he hath dissolved my dignity and humbled me,
And he hath taken away my renown.
He hath opened a way to my miseries;
They enter and no one helpeth me.

CCLV

With rumbling and booming they bounded along;
Terrors are turned upon me;
Thou scatterest my dignity, as with a wind,
And my welfare passeth as a cloud.

CCLVI

The night gnaws away my bones,
And my devourers need no repose;
By swellings is my garment misshapen,
And I am grown like unto dust and ashes.

CCLVII

I cry and thou hearest me not,
Thou art become ruthless towards me;
With the strength of thy hand thou assailest me,
And thou meltest my salvation away.

CCLVIII

For I know that thou wilt bring me to death,
And to the house appointed for all living.
But shall not a drowning man stretch out his hand?
Shall he not cry out in his destruction?

CCLIX

Did I not weep for him that was in trouble?
Was not my soul grieved for the needy?

I looked for good and waited for light :
Behold days of sorrowing are come upon me.

CCLX

I go mourning without sun ;
I stand up in the assembly and cry aloud ;
I am become a brother unto jackals,
And a comrade unto ostriches.

CCLXI

My skin hath grown black upon me
And my bones are scorched with heat ;
My harp is turned to mourning,
And my bagpipe into the wail of the weeping.[1]

CCLXII

If I have walked with men of wickedness,
Or if my feet have hastened to deceit,

---

[1] Two strophes are wanting here, in which Job presumably says that this great change of fortune is not the result of his conduct. The LXX offers nothing here in lieu of the lost verses; but the Massoretic text has the strophes which occur in the Authorised Version (xxxi. 1-4), and which would seem to have been substituted for the original verses. The present Hebrew text is useless here. If the four Massoretic verses which it offers had stood in the original, so important are they that they would never have been omitted by the Greek translators, who evidently did not possess them in their texts. They remind one to some extent of certain passages of the Sermon on the Mount, and are manifestly of late origin.

Let him weigh me in balances of justice,
That God may know mine integrity!

CCLXIII

If my steps have swerved from the way,
And mine heart followed in the wake of mine eyes,
Let me now sow and another eat,
Yea, let my garden be rooted out!

CCLXIV

If mine heart have been deceived by a woman,
Or if I have lain in wait at my neighbour's door,
Then let my wife turn the mill unto another
And let others bow down upon her!

CCLXV

For adultery is a grievous crime,
Yea, a crime to be punished by the judges:
It is a fire that consumeth to utter destruction,
And would root out all mine increase.

CCLXVI

Had I despised the right of my man-servant
Or of my maidservant, when they contended with me,
What could I do, when God rose up?
And when he visiteth, what could I answer him?

CCLXVII

For perdition from God was a terror to me,
And for his highness' sake I could not do such things.
Did not he that made me in the womb, make him?[1]
And did he not fashion us in one belly?

CCLXVIII

Never have I withheld the poor from their desire,
Nor caused the widow's eyes to fail;
Nor have I eaten my morsel alone,
Unless the fatherless had partaken thereof.

CCLXIX

If I saw one perish for lack of clothing,
Or any of the poor devoid of covering;
Then surely did his loins bless me,
And he was warmed with the fleece of my sheep.

CCLXX

If I lifted up my hand against the fatherless,
When I saw my backers in the gate,[2]
Then let my shoulder fall from its setting,
And mine arm from its channel bone!

---

[1] *I.e.*, my servant.

[2] The concourse of people and partisans at the gate where justice was administered.

CCLXXI

I have never made gold my hope,
Nor said to the fine gold: " Thou art my trust ;"
Never did I rejoice that my wealth was great,
And because mine hand had found much.

CCLXXII

Never did I gaze upon the sun, because it shone brightly,
Nor upon the moon floating in glory,
So that my heart was secretly enticed,
And I wafted kisses to them, putting my hand to my mouth.[1]

CCLXXIII

Never did I rejoice at the ruin of my hater,
Nor exult when misery found him out;
Neither have I suffered my throat to sin,
By wreaking a curse upon his soul.

CCLXXIV

Never had the guests of my tent to say :
"Oh, that we had our fill of his meat!"
I suffered not the stranger to lodge out of doors,
But I opened my gates to the traveller.

CCLXXV

I covered not my failings after the manner of men,
By locking mine iniquity in my bosom,

---

[1] *I.e.*, I never adored them as gods.

As if I feared the vast multitude,
Or because the scorn of families.[1] appalled me.

CCLXXVI

And I, forsooth, should keep silence, should not come forward!
Oh, that one would hear me!
Here is my signature; let the Almighty answer me,
And hear the indictment which my adversary hath written![2]

CCLXXVII

Surely I would hoist it upon my shoulder,
And weave it as a crown unto myself;
I would account to him for the number of my steps;
As a prince would I draw near unto him.

CCLXXVIII

JAHVEH:

Who is this that darkeneth my counsel,
With words devoid of knowledge?
Now gird up thy loins like a man,
For I shall ask of thee, and do thou teach me!

---

[1] Of the nobles.
[2] This is the passage become famous in the imaginary form: "That mine adversary had written a book!" (xxxi. 35).

CCLXXIX

When I laid the earth's foundation where wast thou?
Declare, if thou hast understanding!
Who hath laid the measures thereof, if thou knowest,
Or who hath stretched the line upon it?

CCLXXX

Where are its sockets sunk down,
Or who laid the corner-stone thereof?
When the morning stars exulted together,
And all the sons of God shouted for joy.

CCLXXXI

Who shut in the sea with doors,
When it brake forth as issuing from the womb?
When I made the clouds its garment,
And thick darkness for its swaddling-band.

CCLXXXII

Then I brake up for it its appointed place,
And set it bars and portals,
And said: "Hitherto shalt thou come,
And here shall thy haughty waves be stayed!"

CCLXXXIII

Was it at thy prompting that I commanded the morning,
And caused the dawn to know its place?

That it might seize hold of the ends of the earth,
That the wicked might be shaken out?[1]

CCLXXXIV

Then the earth changes as clay under the seal,
And all things appear therein as an embroidery;[2]
But from the wicked is withholden their hiding-place,
And the raised arm shall be shattered.

CCLXXXV

Hast thou entered into the springs of the sea?
Or hast thou walked in search of the abysses?
Have the gates of death been opened unto thee,
Or hast thou seen the doors of darkness?

CCLXXXVI

Hast thou surveyed the breadth of the earth?
Declare, if thou knowest, its measure!
Thou must needs know it, for then wast thou already born,
And great is the number of thy days!

CCLXXXVII

Which way leadeth to the dwelling of light?
And of darkness, where is the abode?

---

[1] Daylight is hostile to criminals, and the manner in which it operates is here compared to a tossing of them off the outspread carpet of the earth.

[2] On a carpet, to which the earth is still compared.

That thou shouldst take it to its bounds,
And that thou shouldst know the paths to its house?

CCLXXXVIII

Hast thou entered into the granaries of the snow,
Or hast thou seen the arsenals of the hail,
Which I have laid up for the time of trouble,
Against the day of battle and of war?

CCLXXXIX

By what way is the mist parted?
And the east wind scattered upon the earth?
Who hath divided its course for the rain-storm?
And its path for the lightning of thunder?

CCXC

Out of whose womb issued the ice?
And who gendered the hoar-frost of heaven?
The waters are as stone,
And the face of the deep condensed like clots together.

CCXCI

Canst thou bind the knots of the Pleiads,
Or loose the fetters of Orion?
Canst thou send lightnings that they may speed,
And say unto thee: Here we are?

CCXCII

Who in his wisdom can number the clouds,
Or who can pour out the bottles of heaven,
That the dust may thicken into mire,
And the clods cleave close together?

CCXCIII

Canst thou hunt its prey for the lion,
Or sate the appetite of the young lions,
When they couch in their dens,
And abide in the covert to lie in wait?

CCXCIV

Who provideth his food for the raven,
When his young ones cry unto God?
It hovereth around nor groweth weary,
Seeking food for its nestlings.

CCXCV

Canst thou mark when the hinds do calve?
Canst thou number the months when they bring forth?
They cast out their burdens,
Their little ones grow up out of doors.

CCXCVI

Who hath sent out the wild ass free,
Whose dwelling I have made the wilderness,

Who scorneth the noise of the city,
Nor heedeth the driver's cry?

CCXCVII

Will the wild ox be willing to serve thee,
Or abide by thy grip?
Wilt thou trust him because his strength is great,
Or wilt thou leave thy labour to him?

CCXCVIII

Dost thou bestow might upon the horse?
Dost thou clothe his neck with a waving mane?
Dost thou make him to bound like a locust,
In the pride of his terrible snort?

CCXCIX

He paws in the vale and rejoices;
Goes with strength to encounter the weapons;
He mocks at fear, and is not dismayed,
And recoileth not from the sword.

CCC

The quiver clangs upon him,
The flashing lance and the javelin;
Furiously bounding, he swallows the ground,
And cannot be reined in at the trumpet-blast.

CCCI

When the clarion soundeth he crieth, "Aha!"
And sniffs the dust raised by the hosts from afar;
He dasheth into the thick of the fray,
Into the captains' shouting and the roar of battle.

CCCII

Doth the hawk fly by thy wisdom,
And spread her pinions towards the south?
She builds her nest on high, dwelling on the rock,
And abideth there, seeking prey.

CCCIII

Will the caviller still contend with the Almighty?
He that reproves God, let him answer!
Wilt thou even disannul my judgment?
Wilt thou condemn me that thou mayst be in the right?

CCCIV

If thou hast an arm like God,
If thou canst thunder with a voice like his,
Deck thyself now with majesty and grandeur
And array thyself in glory and splendour!

CCCV

Scatter abroad the rage of thy wrath,
And hurl down all that is exalted!

The haughty bring low by a glance,
And trample down the wicked in their place!

CCCVI

Hide them together in the dust,
And bind their faces in secret!
Then will I, too, confess unto thee
That thine own right hand can save thee!

CCCVII
JOB:

Behold I am vile, what shall I answer thee?
I will lay mine hand upon my mouth.
Once have I spoken, but I will do so no more,
Yea, twice, but I will proceed no further.

CCCVIII

I know that thou canst do everything,
And that nothing is beyond thy reach;
Hence I say: I have uttered that I understand not,
Things too wonderful for me, which I know not.

CCCIX

I have heard of thee by the hearing of the ear,
But now mine eye hath beheld thee;
Therefore I resign and console myself,
Though in dust and ashes.

EPILOGUE

CHAP. XLII. A.V.]

7 ¶ *And it was* so, *that after the Lord had spoken these words unto Job, the Lord said to Eliphaz the Temanite, My wrath is kindled against thee, and against thy two friends: for ye have not spoken of me* the thing that is *right, as my servant Job* hath.

8 *Therefore take unto you now seven bullocks and seven rams, and go to my servant Job, and offer up for yourselves a burnt offering; and my servant Job shall pray for you: for him will I accept: lest I deal with you* after your *folly, in that ye have not spoken of me* the thing which is *right, like my servant Job.*

9 *So Eliphaz the Temanite and Bildad the Shuhite* and *Zophar the Naamathite went, and did according as the Lord commanded them: the Lord also accepted Job.*

10 *And the Lord turned the captivity of Job, when he prayed for his friends: also the Lord gave Job twice as much as he had before.*

11 *Then came there unto him all his brethren, and all his sisters, and all they that had been of his acquaintance before, and did eat bread with him in his house: and they bemoaned him, and comforted him over all the evil that the Lord had brought upon him: every man also gave him a piece of money, and every one an earring of gold.*

12 *So the Lord blessed the latter end of Job more than his beginning: for he had fourteen thousand sheep, and six thousand camels, and a thousand yoke of oxen, and a thousand she asses.*

13 *He had also seven sons and three daughters.*

14 *And he called the name of the first, Jemima; and the name of the second, Kezia; and the name of the third, Kerenhappuch.*

15 *And in all the land were no women found* so *fair as the daughters of Job: and their father gave them inheritance among their brethren.*

16 *After this lived Job an hundred and forty years, and saw his sons, and his sons' sons,* even *four generations.*

17 *So Job died,* being *old and full of days.*

THE SPEAKER

TRANSLATION OF THE RESTORED TEXT

THE SPEAKER

PART I

I. THESIS: *Vanity of the so-called Absolute Joys of Living.*

I.
1.[1] THE words of the Speaker, the son of David, king in Jerusalem.

2. Vanity of vanities, saith the Speaker, vanity of vanities: all is vanity.

3. What profit hath man of all his toil wherewith he wearies himself under the sun?

4. One generation passeth away and another cometh; the earth alone abideth for ever.

5. The sun riseth and the sun goeth down and panting hasteneth back to his place where he rose.

6. The wind sweepeth towards the south and veereth round to the north, whirling about everlastingly; and back to his circuits returneth the wind.

7. All rivers flow into the sea; yet the sea is not full; whence the rivers take their source, thither they return again.

---

[1] For the convenience of the reader I give the chapters and verses as they are in the ordinary Hebrew Bible, so that they can be found at once in the Authorised Version. The letter *a* after the verse number indicates the first half of that verse, the letter *b* the second half.

> 8. The all is in a never-ceasing whirl,
> No man can utter it in words;
> Rest is not vouchsafed to the eye from seeing,
> Nor unto the ear from hearing.[1]

9. The thing that hath been is the same that shall be, and what befell is the same that shall come to pass, and there is no new thing under the sun. 10. If aught there be whereof one would say, "Lo, this is new!"—it was erstwhile in the eternities that were before us.[2]

11. There is no memory of those that were; neither shall there be any remembrance of them that are to come, among their posterity.

12. I, the Speaker, was king over Israel in Jerusalem, 13. and I set my heart to seek out and probe with wisdom all things that are done under heaven. 14. I surveyed all the works that are wrought under the sun, and behold all was vanity and the grasping of wind.

> 15. That which is crooked cannot be straight,
> Nor can loss be reckoned as gain.

16a. I communed with my heart, saying: Lo, I have gathered great and ever-increasing wisdom, more than all that were before me in Jerusalem. 17. Then I set my

---

[1] The meaning is almost the opposite of that of the Authorised Version. Eye and ear are wearied and bewildered by the incessant whirl of the vast machinery of the universe. *Cf.* Schopenhauer, ed. Grisebach, vol. v. p. 295, § 144. The metre of the strophe is identical with that of the "Poem of Job."

[2] It is interesting and instructive to compare this with the identical doctrine of Buddha, as set forth in the canonical book, "Samyuttaka-Nikayo," vol. i. vii., 2 P, 2 Suttam. It is accessible to most readers in the admirable German translation of Dr. K. E. Neumann, Leiden, 1892. Pp. 156, 157.

heart to learn wisdom and understanding. 16*b*. And my heart discerned much wisdom and knowledge, 17, madness and folly. I realised that this also is but a grasping of wind. 18. For

> In much wisdom is much grief;
> Who increaseth knowledge, increaseth sorrow.

II. 1. I said in my heart: Go to, now, I will try mirth and taste pleasure! But behold, this too was vanity.

> 2. Unto laughter I said: It is mad.
> Unto mirth: What cometh of it?

Proofs of the Vanity of Possession and Enjoyment

(*a*) *Because Enjoyment is Marred by Possession*

II. 3. I cast about me, how I might confer pleasure upon my body—my reason continuing to guide with wisdom the while—and how I might take to folly till I should discern what is good for the sons of men that they should do under heaven during the brief days of their existence. 4. I undertook huge works, I builded me houses, cultivated vineyards. 5. laid out gardens and orchards wherein I planted trees with all kinds of fruits; 6. I dug out reservoirs of water wherewith to water the tree-bearing wood. 7. I got me men slaves and female slaves and had servants born in my house; I likewise owned horned and small cattle, above all that were in Jerusalem before me. 8. I also piled up silver and gold, the treasures of kings and provinces, I gat me men singers and women singers, and the delight of the sons of men, wife and wives. 9. And I waxed great and increased more than all that had been before me in Jerusalem; also my wisdom abode with me. 10. And what thing so ever mine eyes coveted, I kept not from them. I withheld not my heart from any joy; but my heart took pleasure in all my labour, for this only was my portion of all my toil.

11. Then I turned to all my works that my hands had wrought and to the worry wherewith I had wearied myself, and behold, all was vanity and a grasping of wind; and there is no profit under the sun.

V. 10. Whoso loveth silver shall not have joy of silver;[1]
 And he who sets his heart on riches reaps nought therefrom.

This too is vanity.

11. When goods increase, they also are multiplied that devour them, and what profit hath the owner thereof save the gazing thereon with his eyes?

12. Sweet is the sleep of the toiler; but his wealth suffered not the rich man to slumber.[2]

(b) *Because Possession is at best but Fleeting*

V. 13. There is a sore evil which I have witnessed under the sun; riches hoarded up by the owner thereof to his own

---

[1] The Authorised Version has "shall not be satisfied with silver." The meaning is that he who loves silver shall not enjoy the good things it can purchase.

[2] *I.e.*, The care and anxiety which accompany the possession of wealth. The Authorised Version has: "The sleep of a labouring man *is* sweet, whether he eat little or much: but the abundance of the rich will not suffer him to sleep." The Hebrew word *saba'* can

undoing.[1] [For such an one treasures them, spending thereby all his days in worry, vexation, grief, and carking care without gladdening his soul;] 14. then the riches perish by evil mishap, and if that man have begotten a son, there is nothing in his hand.

16*a*. But this likewise is a sore evil: exactly as he came, even so shall he go; 15. naked, as he issued from his mother's womb, must he depart again, nor for all his labour shall he carry away aught that might go with him in his hand. 16*b*. What profit hath he then for having toiled for the wind, 17. and likewise passed all his days in darkness, mourning and much grief, suffering and wrath?

(*c*) *Because the Capacity for Pleasure is hedged round with Conditions*

V. 18. Behold what I have found to be good and beautiful: that a man eat, drink and make merry amid all his labour whereat he striveth under the sun during the brief days of his life which God hath allotted to him; for such is his portion. 19. But that God should enable every man on whom he has bestowed riches and treasures, to enjoy these, and taking his share, to have pleasure in his labour, this is

---

signify both wealth and repletion. Here it manifestly means the former; but some well-intentioned person whose ideas of physiology were defective, having taken it to mean repletion, confirmed his view by interpolating the words: "whether he eat little or much."

[1] Here a portion of the original text has been lost, as is evident from the passage beginning "What profit," two sentences lower down, which sums up the troubles of the rich man and makes them consist not merely in the loss of what he actually possessed, but likewise in the hardships and privations which he endured in order to produce his wealth. I give in brackets the words which Professor Bickell conjecturally supplies in lieu of the lost passage.

itself a gift of God.[1] 20. For then he shall not ponder overmuch on the days of his life, since God approveth the joy of his heart.

VI. 1. But there is an evil which I have seen under the sun, and it weighs heavy upon men : 2. that God bestows upon one riches, wealth and honour, grudging him nought for which his soul yearns, yet permitteth him not to taste thereof, but a stranger enjoyeth it. This is vanity and a sore evil. 3. If such an one should beget even a hundred sons and live many years, but his soul could not revel in bliss then I say, an untimely birth is better off than he. 4. For it came into nothingness, and departed in gloom and its name is shrouded in darkness; 3. not even a sepulchre fell to its lot; 5. moreover, it had not gazed upon, nor known the sun; this latter hath more rest than the former. 6. Yea, though one lived a thousand years twice told, yet had not tasted happiness, must not all wander into one place?[2]

7. All man's toil is for his mouth;
And yet the soul[3] gets not its fill.

---

[1] And therefore extremely doubtful. When Koheleth wishes to express the idea of inexorable law, or Fate, he has recourse to the notion of God.

[2] It is only on earth that one can hope for some approximation to happiness. If we fail to obtain it here—and the odds are very much against us—there is no hereafter to look forward to ; for we *all*—the miserable as well as the fortunate—are drifting steadily into one place—the dreary *Sheol*, where there is no pleasure, no striving, no life.

[3] *I.e.*, not merely, as commentators generally suppose, that desire is not satiated; but that the enjoyment for the sake of which alone we desire life, and toil to sustain it, is never attained. The aim of labour is enjoyment, without which existence is a burden; but the real result of it all is the mere support of life without its redeeming pleasures. *Cf.* Schopenhauer, vol. v. pp. 300, 301.

III. 9. What profit hath the toiler from that whereat he labours? 12. I perceived that for him there is no good other than to eat, drink, and make merry in his life; 13. but even this same that any one may eat, drink, and enjoy himself during all his toil, is for him a gift of God.[1]

Proofs of the Vanity of Knowledge

(a) *Because of its Limitation*

III. 10. I considered the working of the world which God gave unto man as a subject of meditation. 11. Unto their perception he made over the universe and likewise all eternity; yet so that they are unable to discern the work that he worketh from the beginning unto the end.[2]

(b) *From its Depressing Effects as Applied to the Order of the World*

III. 14. I discovered that whatever God doeth is for ever;

---

[1] That is to say, is a very uncertain outlook.

[2] This is a remarkable sentence, which, if it could be supposed to be the fruit of the writer's own speculations, would entitle him to a high place in the Pantheon of speculative philosophers. This proposition, which underlies all Buddhistic doctrines, would be formulated by Kant or Schopenhauer somewhat as follows: Time, space, and causality are given to man as the *a priori* conditions of all thought; they are the stuff his mind is made of. As they are likewise the three ingredients of which the universe is composed, it follows that the world is the web of his own intellect, and, in so far as it is knowable, exists for the intellect alone. That which underlies all the shadows of existence, the one eternal force or will, he never beholds.

nothing can be superadded to it, neither can aught be taken away; and God hath so contrived it that man must fear him.

15. What came into being had been already long before, and what will be was long ago; and God quickeneth the past.

(c) *Because of its Depressing Effects as Applied to Human Life and Conduct*

III. 16. Moreover, I saw, under the sun, in the place of equity iniquity, and in lieu of justice crime. 18. I said in mine heart: It is for men's sake that God should try them and show that they are beasts, they unto themselves. 19. For men are an accident, and the beasts are an accident, and the same accident befalleth them all: as these die even so die those, and the selfsame breath have they all, nor is there any pre-eminence of man above beast;[1] for all is nothingness. 20. All drift into one place; all sprang from the dust, and all turn to dust again. 21. Who knoweth whether the breath of man riseth upwards or whether the breath of the beast sinketh downwards to the earth?

22. And I perceived that other good there is none, save only that man should enjoy himself in his work; for that is his portion. For who can show him what shall become of him after his death?

IV. 1. And again I saw all the oppressive deeds that are wrought under the sun; and behold the downtrodden weep,

---

[1] Schopenhauer would express it thus: Our sources of knowledge —inner and outer observation—are identical with those of animals, the difference consisting in that faculty of imparting to our intuitions the form of abstract ideas.

and none comforteth them; and they endure violence from their tyrants, and none consoleth them. 2. Then I appraised the dead who died long since, as happier than the quick who are yet alive; 3. but luckier than both, him who is still unborn, who hath not yet witnessed the evil doings under the sun.

4. And I saw that all striving and all painstaking in the working of men is but the jealousy of one with another; this too is vanity and the grasping of wind. 5. True,

> The fool foldeth his hands,
> And eateth up his own flesh.

6. And yet better is a handful of quietness than both fists filled with drudgery and the grasping of wind.

7. And again I beheld a vain thing under the sun: 8. one who toileth restlessly without enjoying his riches. For whom do I wear myself out and bereave my soul of pleasure? This too is vanity and irksome drudgery.

II. 12. For what manner of man will he be who shall come after me? 18. Then I loathed all my toil, wherewith I had wearied myself under the sun, in order that I should leave it to one who shall come after me. 19. And who knoweth whether he be a wise man or a fool? Yet shall he have sway over all the fruits of my labour which I have gained by toil and wisdom under the sun; this likewise is vanity. 20. And I turned away to let my heart abandon itself to despair because of the pains wherewith I laboured under the sun. 21. For here is a man who hath performed his work with wisdom, knowledge and painstaking, and to one who hath not laboured thereat he must leave it, as his portion. This also is vanity and a sore evil.

22. For what hath man of all his striving and of the

worry of his heart wherewith he labours under the sun? 23. For all his days are sorrows and his work grief; yea, even at night his heart taketh no rest; this too is vanity.

24. There is no good for man, save that he should eat and drink and make glad his soul in his labour. Yet I saw that even this lieth in the hand of God.' 25. For who can eat and who can enjoy except through him? 26. For on the man who findeth favour in his sight he bestoweth wisdom, knowledge, and joy; but to him who is not pleasing in his sight[2] he giveth drudgery, to gather and to heap up in order to make it over to him in whom he is well pleased. This also is vanity and a grasping of wind.

Proofs of the Vanity of Wisdom in its Religious and Moral Aspects[3]

(a) *Because in the Chances of Life and Death the Just are Nowise Favoured*

II. 12a. Then I turned to behold wisdom, madness and folly, 13. and I saw that wisdom excelleth folly as much as light surpasseth darkness:

---

[1] That is to say, is highly uncertain; for, as we learn in the following lines, happiness and misery depend upon chance or luck. God gives his favourites an agreeable life, leaving the drudgery to all the rest. And his choice is not determined by any ethical acts of man.

[2] "Sinner" is not the correct translation of the Hebrew word *khôte* here; otherwise the author could not say that this too (*i.e.*, the punishment of the sinner) is vanity.

[3] The Jews frequently give to piety and morality the name of wisdom.

14. The wise man hath eyes in his head;
But the fool walketh in obscurity.

But I perceived that the same fate overtaketh them all 15. Then I said in mine heart: As it happeneth to the fool, so shall it happen also unto me; and why then have I been so very wise? Whereupon I said in my heart that this too is vanity. 16. For there is no more remembrance of the wise man than of the fool for ever; because in the days to come all shall have been long since forgotten, and how the wise man perisheth like the fool!

17. Then I loathed life; because the turmoil under the sun weighed upon me as a calamity, for all is vanity and a grasping of wind. III. 1. To everything there is a season and each thing under heaven hath its hour.[1] 2. There is a time to be born and a time to die; a time to plant and a time to pluck up that which is planted; 3. a time to kill and a time to heal; a time to break down and a time to build up; 4. a time to weep and a time to laugh; a time to mourn and a time to dance; 5. a time to cast away stones and a time to gather stones together; a time to embrace and a time to refrain from embracing; 6. a time to seek and a time to throw away; a time to keep and a time to destroy; 7. a time to rend and a time to repair; a time to be silent and a time to speak; 8. a time to love and a time to hate; a time of war and a time of peace. VIII. 6. For every

---

[1] The sense of this passage, which has become proverbial, is generally misunderstood. What it means is that man's work, be he never so skilful, be it never so easy, is absolutely dependent for success upon conditions which are wholly beyond his control, and that undertaken under any other conditions is inevitably doomed to failure.

thing hath its season and its destiny,[1] for the bane of man presses heavily upon him. 7. Because he knoweth not what shall be; for who can tell him how it will come to pass?

> 8. No man swayeth the storm-wind,
> None controlleth the day of his death;
> There is no discharge in war,
> Nor can riches rescue their possessor.

(b) *Because the Just are very often Treated worse than the Wicked*

VIII. 9. All this have I seen, and I have applied my heart unto every event that happens under the sun, at the time when one man ruleth over another to his undoing. 10. And so I beheld the evil-doer honoured, even in the holy place, while they who had done uprightly must go away and were forgotten in the city. This also is vanity.

11. Because sentence against misdeeds is not executed forthwith, therefore the heart of the sons of man is fully set to work evil. 12. For I know that many a miscreant hath committed bad deeds for a protracted time past, and yet lives long, 13. while the God-fearing prolongeth not his shadow-like days.

14. There is a vanity which is done upon earth: to righteous men that happeneth which should befall wrong-doers; and that betideth criminals which should fall to the lot of the upright. I said: This too is vain.

16a. When I applied my heart to know wisdom and to consider the goings on upon earth, 17a. then I perceived

---

[1] Here Professor Bickell supplies the words: "Against this no man can strive."

that no man can find out the whole work of God that is carried on beneath the sun.¹ How much soever he may labour in seeking, he will not discover it; 16*b*. even though by day and by night he should keep his eyes from seeing sleep; 17*b*. yea, though a wise man set himself to fathom it, yet shall he not find it out.²

IX. 1. For all this I laid to heart, and my heart beheld it all; that the righteous and the wise and their doings are in the hand of God; neither love nor hatred doth a man know in advance;³ everything lies before him.

2. All things come alike to all indiscriminately;⁴ the one fate overtaketh the upright man and the miscreant, the clean and the unclean, him who sacrifices and him who sacrifices not, the just and the sinner, him who swears as him who dreads an oath. 3. This is an evil amongst all things that are done under the sun, that one chance betideth all; therefore the sons of men pluck up courage for evil, and madness abideth in their heart.

VIII. 15. Then I commended mirth, because for man there is no good under the sun save only to eat, drink, and make merry, and that abideth with him in his toil during the days of his life which God hath given him under the sun.

---

¹ The utmost that physical science can teach us is the where, the when and the why of the appearance of the forces of nature. The *what* remains for ever a mystery.

² Wisdom here is taken to mean the one eternal reality which underlies the shadowy appearances that we see and know. The same use of the word and exactly the same thesis occur in Job. (*Cf.* A.V. Job xxviii. 21, 22.)

³ He cannot answer even for his own sentiments, completely though they may seem to be under his sway.

⁴ *I.e.*, without ethical distinctions between the good and the bad.

Proofs of the Vanity of Wisdom in its Aspect as Prudence and Practical Aptitude

(a) *Because Success is Contingent upon Circumstances beyond the Control of Man*

IX. 11. Again I saw under the sun that the race is not to the swift, nor the battle to the strong, nor bread to the wise, nor riches to men of understanding, nor favour to men of skill; but time and chance overtake them all. 12. For man knoweth not even his own time; like the fishes that are taken in the evil net, and like the birds that are caught in the snare, so are the sons of men entrapped in the season of misfortune, when it breaks in upon them unawares.[1]

(b) *Because of the Difficulty of obtaining recognition for it, and of the Ease with which it may be Thwarted by Folly*

IX. 13. This also have I seen under the sun, as wisdom, and it appeared great unto me. 14. There was a little city and few soldiers therein, and there came a mighty king against it, and besieged it, and built great bulwarks against it. 15. Now he found in it a poor wise man who, by his wisdom, delivered the city; but no one remembered this poor man afterwards. 16. Thereupon I said:

> Wisdom is better than strength;
> Yet the poor man's wisdom is despised.

---

[1] It is curious to note that a comparison strikingly similar to this occurs in the ancient Indian collection of fables entitled "Pantschatantra." (Ed. Kosegarten, p. 105.)

17. The words of the wise are gently uttered;
   But the clamour of fools is deafening.[1]
18. Wisdom is better than war weapons;
   Yet a single oversight bringeth ruin.
X. 1. A dead fly causes balsam to putrefy;
   So a little folly destroys much happiness.

VI. 8. For what hath the wise more than the fool? What, the poor who knoweth how to walk before the living? 10. That which is happening was long ago named, and it is known beforehand what a man shall be; neither can he join issue with him who is mightier than he. 11. For there is much prattle that only augmenteth vanity. Of what avail is it to man? 12. For who knoweth what is helpful to man in life during the brief vain days of his existence which he spendeth as a shadow? For who can tell a man what shall come to pass after him under the sun?

PART II

RECOMMENDATION OF THE RELATIVE GOOD; AND IN THE FIRST PLACE OF WISDOM, AS RENUNCIATION

(a) *Of Claims to Happiness*

VII. 1a. Better is a good name than choice unguents,
X. 1. But better wisdom than glory;
   [Better not being than existence,[2]]
VII. 1b. And the death-day than the birthday.

---

[1] Literally: tyrannical.

[2] This line is no longer found in the Hebrew or Greek texts. It is required, however, by the sense and metre, and is inserted by Professor Bickell.

2. Better to enter the house of mourning
Than to go into the tavern;
Because there is the end of every man,
And he who survives will lay it to heart.

3. Better is sorrow than laughter;
For a cheerless face makes a blithesome heart.
4. The heart of the wise is in the mourning-house;
The heart of fools in the house of mirth.

5. Better to hearken to the rebuke of the wise,
Than to listen to the song of the foolish.
6. As the crackling of thorns under a pot,[1]
Is the inane laughter of the fool.

VI. 9. Better look with the eyes than wander with desire;
This too is vanity and a grasping of wind.
VII. 7. For extortion maketh the wise man foolish,
And bribery robs understanding.

8. Better the end of a thing than the beginning thereof;
Better is patience than haughtiness.
9. Let not thy spirit be hurried into anger,
For anger lurketh in the bosom of fools.

10. Say not: Why were old times better than these? For it is not from wisdom that thou askest thus.

13. Contemplate the work of God! Who can straighten what he hath made crooked? 14. In the day of prosperity be of good cheer, and in the evil day bethink thee: the latter God hath made even as the former, to the end that man at his death shall have left nothing unaccomplished.

---

[1] Here the Hebrew text contains a play of words which cannot be reproduced in English.

(b) As Renunciation of Reputation for Perfect Justice and Wisdom

VII. 15. All things have I witnessed in my vain days; there are just men who perish through their righteousness, and there are wicked men who prolong their lives by means of their iniquity.[1]

16. Be not righteous overmuch, neither make thyself overwise; why wouldst thou ruin thyself? 17. Do not allow thyself too much liberty, and be not a fool; why wouldst thou die before thy time? 18. It is well that thou shouldst hold fast to the one and also not withdraw thy hand from the other, for he who feareth God compasseth all this.

19. Wisdom is a stronger guard for the wise man than ten mighty men who are in the city.

> 11. Wisdom is good with an inheritance,
> Yea, better yet, to them that see the sun;[2]
> 12. For wisdom and wealth afford shade,
> And wisdom, besides, keeps its possessors alive.

(c) As Renunciation of One's Claims to the Respect and Consideration of Others

VII. 21. Likewise, take not all the gossip of people to heart, lest thou hear that thy friend hath reviled thee! 22. For thy heart is conscious that thou thyself hast oftentimes made little of others. 20. For:

> There is no just man upon the earth
> Who worketh good and never faileth.

---

[1] "Some rise by sin, and some by virtue fall." ("Measure for Measure.") [2] *I.e.*, for mankind.

(d) *Of One's Claims to Act Independently of their Counsel and Aid*

IV. 9. Two are better off than one; 10. for should one of them fall, the other lifts him up again. Woe to him that is alone, if he fall, and there be not another to raise him up. 11. Likewise, if two lie down together, they become warm; but how can one grow warm alone? 12. Moreover, if a man would overpower the single one, two can keep him at bay, and a threefold cord will not easily give way.

13. Better is the youth, needy and wise, than the king old and foolish, who can no longer take a warning to heart. 14. For the former went forth from prison to govern, though born poor in the realm of the king. 15. I saw all the living who walk under the sun, in attendance on the youth who was to take his place. 16. There was no end to the multitude . . . .¹ who were before them; nor did those who lived afterwards glory in him. For this likewise is vanity and a grasping of wind.

RECOMMENDATION OF WISDOM AS RATIONAL PIETY²

A Warning:
(a) *Against Outward and Sacrificial Worship*

V. 1. Keep thy foot when thou goest to the house of God! And to draw near him, in order to obey, is better

---

¹ Here a portion of the text is evidently lost. Professor Bickell suggests that it ran somewhat as follows: "Who received him with applause and reviled the old king. For inasmuch as he had spurned the counsel of the wise, in order to misgovern and grind down the people, therefore they hated him as those had hated him" who were before them.

² As an antidote to the so-called "piety" founded upon the scru-

than the offering of sacrifices by fools : for they know not
.... ¹ to work evil.

(b) *Against Mechanical Prayer*

V. 2. Be not rash with thy mouth, nor let thy heart be hasty to utter words before God ! For God is in heaven, and thou art upon earth ; therefore let thy words be few ! 3. For

> Dreams proceed from much brooding,
> And the prattle of fools from a multitude of words.

(c) *Against Rash Vows*

V. 4. If thou makest a vow unto God, fail not to fulfil it, for fools are displeasing. Carry out that which thou hast promised. 5. It is better thou shouldst not vow at all than vow and not perform. 6. Suffer not thy mouth to render thy body punishable, neither utter thou the plea before the messenger :² "it was rashness." Why cause God to be wroth at thy voice and destroy the work of thy hands ?

---

pulous observance of the law, which had become a very Upas tree of self-complacency. Mankind is already encompassed by so many and such terrible evils, that it would be sheer madness to turn religion into a means of multiplying them.

¹ Another passage is wanting here, which most probably was to the effect that they know not that God asks no sacrifices at their hands but only works of justice ; and that therefore they take courage " to work evil."

² Various commentators have offered various explanations of this obscure passage. As none of them is convincing, I prefer to leave them unnoticed. It is not impossible that it may contain an allusion to some popular tale or fable, analogous to that of the man who called upon death in his despair, and when the grim visitor made his appearance, asked him merely to help him to carry his burden.

(d) *Against Arbitrary Religious Speculations*

V. 7. . . . [1] For in the multitude of fancies and prattle there likewise lurketh much vanity. Rather fear thou God!

RECOMMENDATION OF WISDOM AS ACTIVITY

(a) *In Public Life*

V. 8. When thou witnessest oppression of the poor and the swerving from right and equity in the land, marvel not thereat. For a higher one watcheth over the high, and still higher ones over both.[2] 9. But a gain to the country is only a king—for tilled land.

> X. 16. Wo, land, to thee whose king is a child,
> And whose princes feast in the early morning!
> 17. Hail to thee, land, whose king is noble,
> And whose princes eat in due season!
> 18. Through sloth the rafters give way;
> Through idleness the roof lets in the rain.
> 19. They misuse food and drink for feasting:
> And gold putteth all things in their grasp.
> 20. Even in thy privacy curse not the king,
> Nor in thy bed-chamber the wealthy;
> The birds of heaven might divulge it,
> And the feathered ones might report the word.

---

[1] Professor Bickell supposes that here some words have fallen out, such as: "Brood not over that which is too marvellous and too lofty for thee, neither say of the dreams of thy heart and the babbling of thy lips, 'I have found the knowledge of the Holy One.'"

[2] This passage is a bitterly ironical onslaught on bureaucracy.

(b) *In Private Life*

XI. 1. Send forth thy bread over the surface of the waters, for after many days thou shalt find it again. 2. Divide thy possessions into seven, yea, into eight portions! For thou knowest not what evil may befall the land. 3. If the clouds fill themselves with rain, they discharge it upon the earth; and whether the tree falleth towards the south or towards the north, in the place where it falleth, there shall it abide.

> 6. In the morning sow thy seed,
> And until evening let not thy hand repose.[1]

For thou knowest not which one shall thrive, this or that, or whether they shall both prosper alike.

> 4. He that observeth the wind shall not sow;
> He that watcheth the clouds shall not reap.

5. As thou knowest not the way of the wind, nor the growth of the bones in the womb of the mother, even so, thou canst not fathom the work of God who compasseth everything.

RECOMMENDATION OF WISDOM AS CIRCUMSPECTION

(a) *In our Dealings with Women*

VII. 23. All this have I tried with understanding; I was minded to acquire wisdom, but it remained far from me.

---

[1] This distich is rhymed in Hebrew.

24. Far off is that which is,[1] and deep, deep; who can fathom it?

25. I turned away, and my heart was bent upon understanding, sifting, and seeking the outgrowth of wisdom and knowledge, madness, and folly. 26. Whereupon I found that more bitter than death is woman—that snare whose heart is a net, whose arms are fetters: the God-favoured shall escape her, but the sinner shall be entangled by her.

27. Lo, this have I found, saith the Speaker, piecing one thing with another in order to discover a result: 28. What my soul hath ever sought for, yet never fallen upon, is this: I have discovered one man, among thousands; and of all these there was not one single woman. 29. Behold, this only have I found: that God made men upright, but they go in search of many wiles.

(b) *In our Relations to the Monarch*

VIII. 1. A man's wisdom brightens up his countenance,
And transforms the coarse rancour of his face.
2. The wise man hearkens to the king's command,
By reason of the oath to God.
3. Steer clear of evil causes![2]
For he[3] doeth even what he listeth.
4. Mighty is the word of the monarch;
Who dares ask him: "What dost thou?"[4]

X. 2. The wise man's heart straineth to the right,
The heart of the fool to the left.
3. Even out of doors he lacketh sense,
Saying unto every one: "I am a fool."[5]

---

[1] What Kant would call *das Ding an sich*. Everything we see and know is but appearance. The underlying substance, "that which is," is unknowable.   [2] Political plots.   [3] *I.e.*, the king.
[4] Ironical.   [5] By his unconsidered acts.

4. Though the wrath of the ruler should swell against thee, yet forsake not thy post. For composure avoids grave mistakes.

5. There is an evil which I beheld under the sun, like unto a blunder, proceeding from the ruler!

> 6. Folly is set in high places,
>   The great ones must sit low down;
> 7. Slaves have I beheld on horseback,
>   And princes trudging on foot.

(c) *In the Conditions of Everyday Life*

X. 8. He that diggeth a pit may fall into it; him who breaketh down walls a serpent may sting. 9. Whoso removeth stones may be hurt therewith; he who cleaveth wood may be endangered thereby.

> 10. If the axe be blunt it demands more strength:[1]
>   Only through intelligence doth exertion avail.
> 11. If the serpent bites before the spell,
>   Then bootless is the charmer's art.
>
> 12. Speech from the wise man's mouth is grace,
>   The lips of a fool swallow him up;
> 13. The first words of his mouth are folly,
>   And the end of his talk rank madness.
>
> II. 15. For in self-conceit babbles the fool,[2]
> X. 14a. The silly man multiplieth his words;
> 15. The fussiness of the fool jadeth him,
>   Who knows not yet the way citywards.[3]

---

[1] Literally, "it must be the more lustily wielded."
[2] This line is found only in the Septuagint.
[3] Probably a proverbial way of saying that a man knows nothing.

Exhortation to enjoy Life

X. 14*b*. Man knoweth not what shall come to pass, and who can tell him IX. 3. during his life, what shall befall after his death? Afterwards they go down to the [¹ dead, and there none can tell him aught nor can he apprehend anything. Even could he take it in, it would avail him nothing, for in *Sheol* there is no participation in life]. 4. For whosoever may enrol himself in the company of all the living, can rest content, seeing that a living dog is better than a dead lion, 5. For the living know at least that they shall die, whereas the dead know not anything at all, neither have they any more a reward, for the memory of them is forgotten. 6. As well their love as their hatred and jealousy has long since passed away, neither have they any more a portion for ever in anything that is done under the sun.

> 7. Go, eat thy bread with joy,
> And quaff thy wine with merry heart.

For God hath countenanced beforehand this thy doing. 8. Let thy garments be always white and let thy head lack not ointment. 9. See life with a woman whom thou lovest throughout all the days of thy empty existence which he hath given thee under the sun, during all thy vain days! For that is thy portion in life² and in thy labour which thou takest under the sun. 10. Whatsoever thy hand findeth to do, do that with thy might. For there is no work, nor

---

¹ The words in brackets are supplied conjecturally by Professor Bickell.

² The Authorised Version has "in this life." But it deviates from the Hebrew original.

cogitation, nor knowledge, nor wisdom in the *Sheol*[1] whither thou goest. XI. 7. But sweet is the light and pleasant it is for the eyes to gaze upon the sun. 8. For how many years soever a man may live, he should enjoy himself during them all, and bear in mind the days of darkness that they shall be many. Everything that is to come, is vain.

> 9. Rejoice, young man, in thy youth![2]
> And let thy heart make thee glad!
> And walk in the ways of thine heart,
> And according to the seeing of thine eyes!
>
> 10a. Drive sorrow from thy heart;
> And put away care from thy flesh!
>
> XII. 1a. And bethink thee of thy fountain,[3]
> In the days of thy youth!

XI. 10b. For youth and dawn are fleeting.

> XII. 1b. Dreary days are drawing near,
> And years approach devoid of joy.
> 2. Then darkened shall be sun and moon,
> And clouds come after rain alway.
>
> 3. The keepers of the house[4] shall quake,
> The sturdy ones[5] shall bend themselves;
> Darksome shall the windows[6] be,
> 4. And closed shall be the portals.[7]
>
> The roar of the mill[8] shall be as the sparrows twitter,
> The daughters of song[9] shall bow low;
> 5. Likewise of heights shall they be afraid,
> For dread shall lie in wait.

---

[1] The nether world where the dead are but shadows.

[2] This and the following quatrain are rhymed in the original; as is also the preceding distich.

[3] Thy wife. [4] The arms. [5] The legs. [6] The eyes.
[7] The ears. [8] The voice. [9] The tones.

3. The grinding maids[1] shall leave off work,
5. The almond-tree[2] shall shed its blooms;
   The grasshopper[3] shall be burdened,
   And the caperberry[4] unavailing.

For man goeth to his everlasting home and the mourners are in readiness in the street.

6. Asunder snaps the silver chain;
   Shivered is the golden lamp;
   The pitcher shattered at the brook;
   The scoopwheel falls into the well.

8. O Vanity of Vanities, saith the Speaker; all is vanity![5]

---

[1] The teeth.   [2] The white hair.   [3] Fascinum.   [4] Κρεις.
[5] The epilogue forms no part of the original text.

THE SAYINGS OF AGUR

TRANSLATION OF THE RESTORED TEXT

THE SAYINGS OF AGUR

FIRST SAYING

On God

I

Sentence of the man who has worried himself about God:
I have worried myself about God and succeeded not;
For I am more stupid than other men,
And in me there is no human understanding.
Neither have I learned wisdom,
So that I might comprehend the science of sacred things.

II

Who has ascended into heaven and come down again?
Who can gather the wind in his fists?
Who can bind the waters in a garment?
Who can grasp all the ends of the earth?
Such an one would I question about God: What is his name?
And what is the name of his sons, if thou knowest it?[1]

---

[1] To this and the following Sayings, Agur's orthodox opponent replies thus:

> Every word of God is purified:
> He is a shield to them that put their trust in him.
>
> Add thou not unto his words,
> Lest he reprove thee, and thou be found a liar.

SECOND SAYING

On Four Insatiable Things

There be three things which are never satisfied,
Yea, four exclaim : " It is not enough ! "

Two things have I demanded of thee, O Jahveh,
Deny me them not before I die :

Frivolity and blasphemous words
And negation remove far from me.

Give me neither poverty nor riches ;
Feed me with food suitable for me.

Lest I be sated and deny thee,
And say, Who is the Lord ?

Or lest I be poor and yield to seduction
And offend against the name of my God.

Accuse not a servant to his master,*
Lest he curse thee and thou be found guilty.

There is a bad generation that curses its father
And doth not bless its mother. †

A bad generation which is pure in its own eyes,
And yet is not washed from its filthiness.

A bad generation, how lofty are its eyes !
And how uplifted its eyelids !

A bad generation whose teeth are as swords,
And whose jaw-teeth are as knives

To devour the poor from off the earth,
And the needy from among men.‡

---

* As if Agur were an aristocrat from blind unreasoning sympathy for the heathen aristocracy. Allusion to Agur's 4th Saying.
† Against Agur's 2nd and 3rd Sayings.
‡ Against Agur's 4th Saying.

THE SAYINGS OF AGUR

The Ghoul hath two daughters:
"Give, give!"—the grave and the womb.[1]
The earth is not filled with water,
And the fire sayeth not, "It is enough!"

THIRD SAYING OF AGUR

On Four Inscrutable Things

There be three things too wonderful for me,
Yea, four which I fathom not:
The way of the eagle in the air,
The way of the serpent upon a rock,
The way of a ship amidst the ocean,
And the way of a man with a maid.[2]

FOURTH SAYING

Four Insupportable Things

Under three things the earth quakes,
And under four it cannot stand.
Under a slave when he seeks to reign,
And under a fool when he is filled with meat;

---

[1] *I.e.*, birth and death. (*Cf. Agur, the Agnostic*, pp. 139, 140.) The champion of orthodoxy evidently took the passage literally and consequently condemned Agur as guilty of a lack of filial respect for his mother, venting his feelings in the following lines:—

"The eye that scoffeth at the grey hair of the father
And that despiseth the old age of the mother,

The ravens of the valley shall pick it out
And the young eagles shall devour it."

[2] Verse 20 A.V. is an addition inserted by a later writer who having misunderstood the last line of the fourth sentence, deemed it his duty to give it a moral turn.

Under an odious woman when she gets a husband,
And under a handmaid who is heir to her mistress.[1]

FIFTH SAYING

Four who stride majestically

There be three things which go well,
Yea, four are comely in going:
A lion—the hero among beasts,
Who turneth not aside for any one;
A greyhound and a bell-goat,
And a king who riseth up for his people's sake.

SIXTH SENTENCE

Exhortation to denounce ambition

Whether thou hast acted foolishly in exalting thyself,
Or whether thou hast done wisely, lay thy hand upon
    thy lips![2]
For pressure of milk produces butter,
And pressure of vanity produces anger;
Pressure of the nose[3] produces blood,
And pressure of wrath produces strife.

---

[1] The Sentence following (vv. 24-24 A.V.) dealing with Four Cunning Ones is probably not from Agur's pen; for not only has it five distichs, but it lacks the point which characterises his Sayings, besides which it does not begin, as his "numerical" Sentences do, with *three* before proceeding to *four*.

[2] Keep silence.

[3] In Hebrew the same word signifies "nose" and "strife."

INDEX

INDEX

ADVERSARY, the, "a son of God," 12
Agur, the Sayings of—
    their literary place, 8
    character of, 133, 134
    their position in Proverbs, 135, 136
    their present form, 137
    Agur and his orthodox opponent, 138, 139
    blunders of the latter, 140, 141
    Oriental influence traceable in the Sayings, 139, 140, 149, 155, 156
    the mystery of generation, 142–144
    date of composition, 147, 148
    Agur shows no respect for the doctrine of retribution, for Messianism, revelation, &c.; no belief in a personal God, 151
    his antagonism to Jewish theologians, 152, 153
    his views of right conduct, 154
Angels, 167
Animals, the tenderness of Buddhism towards, 126, 128
Aryans and Semites, contrast of mental characteristics, 3
Asterisks, Origen's, in the Hexapla, 50
Authorship of Job, 35–37

BICKELL, Professor, and the laws of Hebrew metre, 47
    discovery of the Saïdic version of Job, 51, 52
    on the theophany in Job, 83
    theory as to the chaotic state of Koheleth, 92–94
    and the "Praise of Wisdom," 135
    textual conjectures, 215, 245, 252, 255 n^*, 258 n^1, 260 n^1, 264 n^1
"Book, That mine adversary had written a," 228 n
Book of Job (*see* Job)
Buddhism and the theology of Job, 26–34
    and Job's moral system, 65
    influence of, on Koheleth, 7, 122–128, 242 n^2, 247 n^2, 254 n

INDEX

Buddhism, spread of, into Syria, Egypt, &c., 124-129
    influence of, on Agur, 149, 151, 155, 156
    and the doctrine of Renunciation, 113
    its tenderness towards animals and plants, 126-128
Byron's " Cain " and Job, 45

" CAIN " (Byron's) and Job, 45
" Canticles of Scepticism," Heine's description of Koheleth, 119
Cheyne, Prof., and the date of Job, 37 ;
    and the laws of Hebrew metre, 47 ;
    and Prof. Bickell's theory of the plan of Koheleth, 92 ;
    on the " theism " of Koheleth, 120 n ;
    Job, strophe liii. and Ps. viii. 5 compared,
Christ and the doctrine of Renunciation, 113
Christianity not incompatible with Koheleth's scepticism, 110
Clement of Alexandria and a lost version of Job, 48 n
Cornill, Dr., and the date of Job, 39
Council of Constantinople and the historical truth of Job, 48 n
Critical apparatus applied to text of Job, 46-52

DATE of Job, 37-39, 194 n
    of earliest extant MS. of Job, 43
    of Koheleth, 122 n, 129
    of the Sayings of Agur, 147, 148

ECCLESIASTES (*see* Koheleth)
Ecclesiasticus, dropped leaves causing transposition of chapters in, 93
Elephantiasis, 173 n
Eternal justice, Job's belief in, 66
    Koheleth's belief in, 113
Evil (*see* Good and Evil)
Ewald and the laws of Hebrew metre, 47

FIRMAMENT, the, 178 n
Free-will and the origin of evil, 24, 25
Future life, Job knows nothing of, 11, 16, 17-19
    Koheleth knows nothing of, 112, 121

GHOUL, the (*Tanha*), 140, 149
Good and Evil, problem of, 12-15 ; free-will and the origin of evil, 24, 25 ; the Oriental theory of, 26-30
Gregory the Great and the Book of Job, 5

INDEX

HEBREW metre, Prof. Bickell and the laws of, 47
Heine and the "Canticles of Scepticism," 119
Hitopadeça, the, and the Sayings of Agur, 149

INSPIRATION of Job not affected by reconstructive changes, 55, 56 *n*
Interpolations in Job, examples of, 53–59
Isaac of Antioch, transpositions in poems caused by dropped leaves, 93

JESUS Sirach and the Book of Proverbs, 147, 148
Job, the Poem of—
    compared with Lucretius, *De Nat. Rerum*, 4
    its inclusion in the Canon, 4 *n*
    its appeal to all ages, 5
    opinion of Gregory the Great, Thomas Aquinas, Tennyson, Luther, 5
    its place in literature, 6

    the problem of, 9, 10
    traditional theology, 11
    the mystery of good and evil, 12–15
    no conception of a future life, 11, 16–18
    nor of the Resurrection or Atonement, 16–19
    the poet's view of the problem, 21–23
    free-will and the origin of evil, 24, 25
    the Oriental theory of these, 26–30,
    Brahmanism and Buddhism, 30–32
    Job's illumination the same as Buddha's, 32–34

    authorship of, 35–37
    date of, 37–39, 194 *n*
    the question of historicity, 40, 41
    date of earliest extant MS. of, 43
    a lost version of 48 *n*
    various causes for changes in text, 44
    the chief cause, a horror of blasphemy, 45
    apparatus for detecting these changes, 46–52
    laws of Hebrew metre, 47
    parallelism, 48
    evidence of the Septuagint, 48, 49
    Theodotion's version of the Old Testament, 50
    the Hexapla, 50
    the Saïdic or Thebaic version of Job, 51, 52

INDEX

Job, the Poem of—
    examples of interpolations, 53-59
    reconstructive changes do not affect inspiration, 55, 56 *n*
    Job's natural philosophy, 61, 62
    his dynamic theory of the Universe, 63
    his monotheism not Jewish, 64
    his moral system, based on pity, found in Buddhism, and here first preached in the Old Testament, 65
    belief in eternal justice, 66
    the secret of Job's resignation, 67

    the ancient legend of Job, use of it by the poet, 69, 70
    analysis of the Poem, 71-84
    the appearance of Jehovah not literal, 82
    but symbolical of Job's illumination, 83
Judaism, the influence of Buddhism on, 128, 129

KANT and Koheleth, 7, 247 n^2, 262 n^1
Koheleth—
    its inclusion in the Canon, 4 *n*
    the literary problem of, 7
    its metaphysical basis the same as that of the philosophy of Buddha, Kant, and Schopenhauer, 7

    chaotic and conflicting character of text, 87, 89
    Prof. Bickell's theory as to the confusion of the book, 92-94
    instances of similar confusion in other works, 93
    the proposed re-arrangement, 94, 95 *n*
    illustrations in support of Prof. Bickell's theory, 95-97

    Koheleth's theory of life, 99
    source of happiness not wealth, 100
        nor wisdom, 101, 102
        nor virtue, 103
    Koheleth's system, 105
    relation of God to man, 106
    the practical moral, 107
    the view of " moral order," 109
    the world all Maya, illusion, 110
    Koheleth's theory not inconsistent with Christianity, 110
    the reach of our knowledge; happiness the only true good, 111
    Koheleth knows nothing of future life or of divine promises or revelations, 112

INDEX

Koheleth—
    his belief in eternal justice, 113
    renunciation, the great doctrine, 113, 116
    wisdom the great boon, 114
    content and moderation the golden rule, 115
    the sources of his philosophy, 117
    opposition of Jewish orthodoxy to the book, 118
    admission of the book to the Canon, 118, 119
    its incompatibility with Messianic hopes of Israel, 119
    disbelief in a personal God, 120
        in retribution and immortality, 121
    Greek influences questioned; probable influence of Buddhism, 122-128
    date and locality of Koheleth, 129

LIFE to come (*see* Future Life)
Lucretius compared with Job, 4
Luther and the Book of Job, 5

MAGICIANS mentioned in Job, 163
Maya, illusion, the teaching of Koheleth, 110
Metre in Hebrew, laws of, 47

NIRVANA, Koheleth's only real good, 111
    view of, 126 *n*

OLD Testament, untrustworthiness of historical books, 3
Origen and the Hexapla, 50

PARALLELISM in Hebrew poetry, 48
Paul, St., and a lost version of Job, 48 *n*
"Praise of Wisdom," its place in "Proverbs," Prof. Bickell's discovery, 135
Priests' Code, the, 45 *n*
"Proverbs," analysis of, 133
    not written by Solomon, 134
    their history, 135
    date of, 147
Plants, tenderness of Buddhism towards, 128

RENUNCIATION, the teaching of Koheleth, Buddha, Christ, etc., 113
Resurrection, the (in Job), 16-19
"Redeemer liveth, I know that my," 16-19, 204

SAIDIC or Thebaic version of Job, 51, 52
Sariputto, and the desire for life *(tanha)*, 149, 150
Satan, "a son of God," 12
Scotus Erigena and free-will, 25
Schopenhauer and Koheleth, 7, 101 *n*, 247 *n*²
    and Renunciation, 113
    and the four things insatiable, 140
Semites, remains of ancient speculation among, 4
    and Aryans, contrast of mental characteristics, 3
Septuagint, the value of, in regard to text of Job, 48, 49

TANHA, the terrible Ghoul, 140, 149
Tennyson's opinion of Job, 5
Thebaic or Saidic version of Job, 51, 52
Theodore of Mopsuestia condemned for declaring Job to be fiction, 40
Theodotion's version of the Old Testament, 50
Thomas Aquinas on Job, 5
Transmigration of souls, 30

VEDA, the, 31
Vedanta, the, 31
Vowel points in Hebrew, 138, 139 *n*

" WISDOM, Praise of," its place in " Proverbs," Prof. Bickell's discovery, 135

www.ingramcontent.com/pod-product-compliance
Lightning Source LLC
Chambersburg PA
CBHW031331230426
43670CB00006B/305